Teacher's Lesson Plan Manual
for
The Prophets: Speaking Out for Justice

26 Ready-to-Use Lesson Plans

Includes over 60 ways to use the Internet, Web pages, and Wikispaces to deepen understanding, and to add creativity, interactivity, and excitement to your lessons.

By Ellen J. Rank

RATNER MEDIA AND TECHNOLOGY CE...
JEWISH EDUCATION CENTER OF CLEVELA...

Book and Cover Design: Susan Honeywell, LJ Graphics
Project Editor: Terry S. Kaye

Copyright © 2010 Behrman House, Inc.
Springfield, New Jersey
www.behrmanhouse.com
ISBN: 978-0-87441-601-5
Manufactured in the United States of America

Behrman House, Inc.
www.behrmanhouse.com
www.thejewishprophets.com

```
RMC      Rank, Ellen
223      The prophets
GEV      speaking out
19670    for justice
```

Contents

Introduction 3
Structure of This Lesson Plan Manual 3
Using This Lesson Plan Manual 4
Teaching Strategies 5
Being Inclusive 6
The Tech Connection 7
Parashah References 9

Lesson Plans

Chapter 1 Introduction 10
Chapter 2 Moses: Radical Shepherd of Israel 11
              Lesson 1 12
              Lesson 2 13
               Lesson 3 14
              Lesson 4 15
Chapter 3 Samuel: Reluctant Kingmaker 16
              Lesson 1 17
              Lesson 2 18
              Lesson 3 19
              Lesson 4 20
Chapter 4 Elijah: Zealous Critic of the King 21
              Lesson 1 22
              Lesson 2 23
              Lesson 3 24
              Lesson 4 25
Chapter 5 Amos: Faithful Friend of the Covenant 26
              Lesson 1 27
              Lesson 2 28
              Lesson 3 29
Chapter 6 Isaiah: Righteous Spirit of Worship 30
              Lesson 1 31
              Lesson 2 32
              Lesson 3 33
              Lesson 4 34
Chapter 7 Jeremiah: Persistent Voice of Teshuvah 35
              Lesson 1 36
              Lesson 2 37
              Lesson 3 38
Chapter 8 Jonah: Runaway Messenger of Mercy 39
              Lesson 1 40
              Lesson 2 41
              Lesson 3 42

Constructing Personal Meaning from The Prophets: Speaking Out for Justice 43
Assessments 44

Introduction

The Prophets: Speaking Out for Justice invites students in grades 6 and 7 to find personal meaning in the words and accounts of Israel's most important prophets. Each chapter leads students to consider how the biblical prophets inspire us to speak out in the name of justice.

As students prepare to become b'nai mitzvah, it is fitting for them to study the role of the prophets and how their words are relevant to us today. Many b'nai mitzvah will chant a *Haftarah*—a selection from the books of the Prophets related to their Torah portion—and may offer a *d'var Torah* about the prophet as part of their bat or bar mitzvah ceremony. Thus, students will find the information in *The Prophets: Speaking Out for Justice* personally helpful in preparing for this important milestone.

There are eight chapters in *The Prophets: Speaking Out for Justice*: an introductory chapter and one chapter for each of the great prophets of Israel—Moses, Samuel, Elijah, Amos, Isaiah, Jeremiah, and Jonah.

Each chapter includes these features:

- An **opening drama** recounting the prophet's first encounter with God and additional **dramatic vignettes**. Many of these accounts are a retelling based on the biblical text. Some of the accounts, described as "inspired by," are interpretations of the biblical texts written as modern midrash.

- **Quotes** from the books of the prophets.

- **Prophet's Profile,** which lists basic background information on the prophet, including birth and family information, the prophet's Hebrew name and its meaning, and the prophet's major contribution. Also included are fun facts, such as a favorite quote by the prophet.

- **Prayer Connection** presents a liturgical connection to the teachings of the prophet.

- **Historical Maps** illustrate cities and countries referred to in the chapter.

- **In the Footsteps of the Prophets** presents a modern personality whose actions reflect the values of the prophet.

In addition, the following features appear in several chapters:

- **What Do You Think?** asks open-ended questions related to the actions or words of the prophets.

- **Historical Notes** provide historical background to help students gain a better understanding of the political situation at the time of the prophet.

- **Let's Make a Midrash** invites students to create their own midrashic interpretation of a specific event in the life of the prophet.

Structure of This Lesson Plan Manual

This Lesson Plan Manual presents 26 ready-to-use lesson plans of approximately 50–60 minutes each for *The Prophets: Speaking Out for Justice*. It includes suggestions for teaching every element of the student text. In addition, ideas on how to incorporate technology are included in this introduction (page 7) and in the overview of each chapter.

Each chapter in this manual corresponds to a chapter in the textbook and includes the following elements:

I   An introductory page that presents

- **Chapter Overview** A brief summary of the life and key teachings of the prophet.
- **Core Concepts** A listing of the chapter's central ideas.
- **Learning Objectives** Goals for students to achieve by the end of the chapter.
- **Materials Needed** Useful materials for class activities and discussions.
- **The Tech Connection** Suggestions for using the Internet and for creating student work to be included in a class Web page or Wikispace.

II   Three or four lesson plans that each include

- **Essential Question** An overarching question, one that we may ask at different times in our lives, that reflects the main idea of the lesson.
- **Getting Started** A set induction to get students thinking about the ideas they will learn in that lesson.
- **Exploring the Text** A step-by-step guide for presenting the lesson, including suggested questions and activities and the approximate time for each segment of the lesson.
- **Wrapping It Up** A short activity or discussion to review and reflect on the main ideas presented in the lesson.

In addition to lesson plans, the manual provides open-ended as well as "fact" questions to use for formal assessment. These questions appear at the end of the lesson plan manual (see page 44) and involve some recall of details but focus largely on the big ideas, themes, concepts, and understandings students learn from the words and actions of the prophets.

Using This Lesson Plan Manual

At the start of the year, map out when you plan to teach each chapter. The 26 lessons in the manual have been designed so that you can teach an average of one lesson a week. Heighten student interest and engagement by scheduling additional time for incorporating technology into the study of the prophets.

As you prepare each lesson, remember that the Big Idea of *The Prophets: Speaking Out for Justice* is that **the biblical prophets inspire and teach us to speak out in the name of justice today**. Each lesson should provide students with new opportunities to deepen their understanding of the prophets and how the prophets continue to inspire us to build a better world.

Before you begin to teach a textbook chapter, read through the Lesson Plan Manual to familiarize yourself with the chapter. You may choose to use the lessons exactly as they are, or you may adapt the lessons to fit the needs of your students. If you adapt the lessons, it is important to frame your lesson around an essential question—either the one suggested for the lesson or another one that points to the main idea of the lesson.

The manual is easy to use with the student text. All references to maps, photographs, and readings are in bold, followed by the page number. For example, Lesson 2 of Chapter 2 recommends: Students read **Moses Discovers the Force of Justice and Compassion** (page 10) with a partner.

Teaching Strategies

Opening Rituals

1. Consider beginning each lesson with an opening ritual that signals to students that they are about to study an important text. A lovely and fitting ritual is to recite the blessing for engaging in learning holy texts:

בָּרוּךְ אַתָּה, יְיָ אֱלֹהֵינוּ, מֶלֶךְ הָעוֹלָם, אֲשֶׁר קִדְּשָׁנוּ בְּמִצְוֹתָיו וְצִוָּנוּ לַעֲסוֹק בְּדִבְרֵי תוֹרָה.

Praised are You, Adonai our God, Ruler of the world, who makes us holy with commandments and commands us to study words of Torah.

2. Do a brief review of the previous lesson. You may want to pre-assign students to be responsible for presenting a very short summary of the main ideas discussed. Alternatively, have a few students share their responses to the Essential Question raised in the previous lesson.

3. Post the Essential Question for the lesson to be studied on the board. Invite a volunteer to read aloud the Essential Question. Briefly discuss the meaning of the question, making sure students understand it.

Interpersonal and Intrapersonal Learners

Some students learn best through interacting with others (interpersonal); some learn best independently (intrapersonal). With this in mind, there are suggestions in the lesson plans for independent work and for activities and discussions with a partner, group, or the whole class. In general, if the manual does not specify that students are meeting with a partner or in a group, plan to have a class discussion.

Group Work

Many of the lessons include suggestions for group work. Whenever possible, plan ahead how you want to form the groups. It is important to change the composition of your groups. For some tasks you will want students with a variety of talents and interests. For others you may choose to group together students with similar skills.

Group work is most successful when every group member knows his or her responsibilities. To help make the group's task clear, prepare written instructions before the class. Many of the lesson plans include such instructions. In addition, you may wish to create index cards that describe the jobs of group members. Jobs will vary depending on the type of group work. Some possible jobs include the following:

- Recorder—records the group's suggestions or findings.
- Reporter—reports the group's work to the class.
- Illustrator—draws the group's ideas to present to the class.
- Encourager—encourages group members to stay on task.
- Reader—reads aloud information to the group.

Consider laminating the job description cards and distributing them each time you do group work.

Reading the Text

The lesson plans expect students to spend little time reading the text aloud in class. Be mindful, however, of students who are aural learners. To best understand the material, they will need to hear the information. In such cases, you may adapt the lessons so that the students hear the text. You might, for example, have partners quietly read a short section of text aloud to one another.

Student Notebooks

The lessons frequently include activities that require students to write responses to questions before they share their answers with a partner, group, or the class. If possible, each student should have his or her own notebook that you keep in the classroom and distribute when teaching a lesson in which students will need to write responses. These notebooks will also serve as informal journals of students' thoughts about the teachings of the prophets and records of students' work.

Bar and Bat Mitzvah Parashah

At the start of the year, ask each student to write down when she or he will become a bat or bar mitzvah, and the Torah portion and *Haftarah* that will be read on that day. (You may wish to double-check the congregation's calendar.) Have the students create a poster that lists each of their names along with their Torah portion and *Haftarah* reading.

Use the list of references (page 9) throughout the year to identify when the class is learning something relevant to a student's bat or bar mitzvah reading. Students may find references to their Torah portion in the chapter on Moses and references to their *Haftarah* readings in the chapters on Samuel, Elijah, Amos, Isaiah, or Jeremiah. Consider having students record on the poster the page numbers from the student text that correspond to their readings.

Being Inclusive

Like most classes, yours probably includes a diverse group of learners. To succeed, some students may require a variety of strategies or additional attention. The activities in this manual are intended for a wide spectrum of learners and therefore employ a variety of modalities. In general, teachers who present material in many different ways will be able to reach many more children.

It is always helpful to find out from parents what accommodations, if any, their child's secular school makes. In addition, consider using one or several of the strategies below when you think they can address a particular learning need.

- Mask parts of the textbook page so that only the activity being taught is visible. This can reduce distractions for some students and help them focus on the key lesson content.

- Highlight the information in the text to which students should pay close attention.

- Help students share what they know in ways that are compatible with their learning styles. For example, where appropriate, allow students to answer questions orally instead of writing their answers.

- Invite students to paraphrase and summarize what they have learned. This is helpful for all students.

- Allow extra time for students who need it to finish assignments, or reduce the number of items you expect students to complete.

- Repeat and define new words and concepts several times. Do not assume that all students will recognize them when they see or hear them again later in the class session or the following week.

- If students have trouble pronouncing new vocabulary, especially in Hebrew, model the words and have students repeat them after you.

- Create flashcards with key vocabulary words or concepts on one side and definitions on the other. Invite children to take the cards home and practice with a parent.

- Set up all students to succeed. When assigning small groups, make sure every student can make a contribution to the group. If that is not possible, adapt the learning experience for students with specific learning needs.

- Reach out to your director of education for suggestions and guidance.

Most important, remember that the interpersonal relationships you build and the tone and atmosphere you create in your classroom are as important as the material you teach. At all times, try to model and encourage the qualities of patience and tolerance in all of your students.

When we interact compassionately and justly with our students, we are bringing to life the teachings of the prophets.

The Tech Connection

Your students are growing up in a world in which using technology is part of their daily lives at home and at school. There are infinite ways that you can take advantage of the Internet and digital applications to deepen understanding, and to add creativity, interactivity, and excitement to your lessons.

With your students visit the Behrman House site www.thejewishprophets.com, where you will find additional material to deepen students' understanding of the prophets. The site is envisioned as a place for the student to do a little additional research, perhaps for a *d'var Torah* on their *parashah*, using the links to the Mitzvah Machine on www.babaganewz.com; find ideas for service projects; and explore additional biographies of people who exemplify the values of each prophet. There are also entries for each prophet from the textbook (each prophet has a Facebook-like page).

In addition, there is a section called "Where are the women?" with information on Miriam, Hannah, the midwives, and Deborah, along with the names of Torah portions in which these women are mentioned. An introductory paragraph discusses the lack of women prophets in biblical times.

Look for prompts throughout the student text directing you to this site.

Send your students only to Web sites you have already visited and approved. If you have a SMART Board™ check the Internet for lesson plans and activities for using the SMART Board™ to make lessons even more engaging and interactive.

Another way to take advantage of computer technology is to create a Web site or Wikispace devoted to *The Prophets: Speaking Out for Justice*. If your congregation already has a Web site, find out if your class can have a space on it. Alternatively, there are instructions on the Internet for setting up your own Web site or Wikispace.

Use the class Web site or Wiki as an anchor activity throughout the year. An anchor activity is an ongoing project directly related to the curriculum that students can work on independently. Students might work on the Web site if they arrive early to school or are the first to finish a class assignment, or while you are working with another group of students. You might also designate class time when everyone works on projects that will be posted to the Web site.

The following suggestions will help you use technology in a variety of ways:

- Upload photographs of your students engaged in activities from the lesson plans in this manual.
- Post a survey question for parents based on a value in the chapter, then tally and share the results.
- List the students who have verses from the chapter in their bar or bat mitzvah portion.
- Post students' responses to open-ended questions from the text or to Essential Questions.
- Set up a class blog. Students can write their reactions to events recounted in the chapter.
- Design a timeline. Add to the timeline after you complete each chapter.
- Have students rewrite the words of the prophets using texting shorthand ("net lingo"), for example, brb, lol.
- Upload maps of where the prophets lived and traveled.
- Write an interview with a prophet—What would the prophet tell us today? What would the prophet be proud of when looking at today's Jewish community?
- Upload original artwork created by students depicting events in the chapter. Students can write what they learn from the art.
- Compile a list of Jewish organizations that help Jews and non-Jews, especially organizations in which students are themselves involved. Include news reports of acts of kindness, such as the IDF (Israel Defense Forces) helping victims of disasters in other countries.

Start the year by having students make a list of suggestions of ways they can use the Internet—and their mobile devices—to bring the material to life. Keep this list handy and implement their suggestions throughout the year.

Parashah References

Below is a listing of biblical verses that are quoted, paraphrased, or referenced in *The Prophets: Speaking Out for Justice*. Use this list to help students connect the Torah (T) and *Haftarah* (H) readings from their bar and bat mitzvah to your lessons in class.

Chapter	Page	Biblical Source	Parashah
1	5	Deuteronomy 5:24	Va'ethanan (T)
2	8; 9	Exodus 3–4; 2:10	Sh'mot (T)
2	9; 14; 16	Exodus 20:3; 18:25–26; 19:4-8	Yitro (T)
2	12; 14	Exodus 15:11; 15, 16, and 17	B'shalah (T)
2	15	Exodus 9:1	Va'eira (T)
2	17	Exodus 34:29–30	Ki Tisa (T)
2	18	Exodus 22:25–26	Mishpatim (T)
2	18	Deuteronomy 10:18–19	Eikev (T)
2	18	Leviticus 19:14	K'doshim (T)
2	18	Deuteronomy 34:10	V'zot Habrachah (T)
3	20	1 Samuel 1:9–3:10	First day of Rosh Hashanah (H)
3	23	Judges 4:4–5; 5:4–5; 5:8	B'shalah (H)
4	34	Genesis 1	B'reishit (T) Simchat Torah
4	35; 39 and 40	I Kings 18:18; 18:21–39	Ki Tisa (H)
5	46; 50; 52	Amos 3:7–8; 2:6–7, 2:12; 3:2	Vayeishev (H)
5	57	Deuteronomy 16:20	Shoftim (T)
6	58 and 63; 68	Isaiah 6; Exodus 20:3	Yitro (H); (T)
6	58	Isaiah 1	D'varim (H)
6	62	Leviticus 19:17–18	K'doshim (T)
6	64; 65	Isaiah 40:28–29; 40:27	Lech L'cha (H)
6	64	Isaiah 42:6–7	B'reishit (H)
6	65	Isaiah 11:12	Eighth day of Passover (H)
6	68	Isaiah 44:6	Vayikra (H)
6	68	Isaiah 40:4–5	Va'etchanan (H)
6	69	Deuteronomy 16:20	Shoftim (T)
7	70	Jeremiah 1:4–10	Mattot (H) Sh'mot (H)
7	72	Numbers 14:10	Sh'lah (T)
7	79	Jeremiah 17:14	B'hukkotai; B'har-B'hukkotai (H)
8		Jonah 1–4	Minhah of Yom Kippur (H)
8	88	Numbers 20:7–11	Hukat (T)

Chapter 1
Introduction

Getting Started: (5 minutes) Write "The Prophets: Speaking Out for Justice" on the board. Discuss the meaning of the title. Students give examples of what it means to speak up for justice. Ask students for the names of any prophets they know and list them on the board. Tell students that this year they will study seven major prophets of Israel who inspire us to speak up for justice, honor Jewish values, and build a better world.

Exploring the Text:

1. (10 minutes) Give each student a copy of *The Prophets: Speaking Out for Justice*. Allow students time to page through the book and name the prophets they will learn about this year. Point out common features that appear in the chapters. Clarify that the accounts of Moses are found in the first part of the Tanakh—the Torah—and that the accounts and writings of the six other prophets are found in the second part of the Tanakh—Nevi'im, the books of the Prophets.

2. (5 minutes) Students read silently the **first paragraph** on page 4. Ask questions, guiding students to understand the origin of reading the *Haftarah*. A volunteer reads the caption below the **photo of the girl** (page 5). Students name the *Haftarah* they will chant when becoming a bar or bat mitzvah.

3. (15 minutes) A student reads aloud the caption next to the **photo of the road sign** (page 5). Students suggest why a modern street would be named after the prophets. Point out to students the similarities between the name of the street and the terms introduced on pages 5–7 (*n'vu'ah, navi, divrei n'vi'ut, and Ha-Nevi'im Street*). Divide the class into three groups. Assign each group the job of defining one of the terms and explaining it to the class. Note: Consider summarizing the main points of this information to your students.

4. (5 minutes) Students read silently the caption next to the **photo of the teenagers** (page 6). Describe how technology will be incorporated into the study of the prophets. If you have access to the Internet, go to www.thejewishprophets.com and have your students explore some of its components.

5. (5 minutes) Partners read **Know Your BCEs!** (page 6). Partners calculate how many years have passed since Amos prophesied in 750 BCE [current year + 750 = x]. Also ask them to calculate how many years have passed since the Second Temple was destroyed in 70 CE [current year − 70 = x]. On the board, write "Torah," "Nevi'im," and "Ketuvim" in a column. A volunteer circles the T, N, and K and explains how these letters form the word *TaNaKh*.

> **Wrapping It Up:** (5 minutes) Students read silently **The Age of Prophecy** (page 7). A volunteer reads aloud the last sentence. As a class, discuss what it means to be God's partner. Remind students that while the teachings of the prophets are ancient, they are still relevant. Students brainstorm a list of values and teachings that were as true two or three thousand years ago, in the days of the prophets, as they are today.

Chapter 2
Moses: Radical Shepherd of Israel

Chapter Overview Beginning in his infancy, Moses experiences great deeds of compassion. His life is spared by the actions of the midwives, his mother, his sister, and Pharaoh's daughter. Moses, a shepherd, hears Adonai call out to him from a burning bush that is not consumed. Adonai charges Moses to go to Pharaoh and lead the Israelites out of Egypt, from slavery to freedom. Despite Moses's uncertainty of his own qualifications, Moses accepts God's command and leads the people with justice and compassion. As the Israelites face difficulties in the desert, they lose faith in God. Yet Moses continues to lead them and prepare them to be a "kingdom of priests and a holy nation." Moses gives the Israelites active roles in a new judicial system. After journeying in the desert for three months, the Israelites assemble at Mount Sinai and, through Moses, receive God's commandments and accept God's Covenant. Like the Israelites who left Egypt, we are "a kingdom of priests" obligated to perform acts of kindness, truth, and justice.

Core Concepts
- The Jewish people have had a Covenant with God for thousands of years.
- From the Torah we learn that we must act with compassion, truth, and justice.
- Moses was the greatest of all the prophets.

Learning Objectives Students will be able to:
- Describe the qualities of a good leader and Moses's own leadership qualities. (Lesson 1)
- Retell biblical and rabbinic accounts that reflect the importance of compassion. (Lesson 2)
- Suggest what it felt like to journey through the desert, why it was challenging to balance freedom and faith, and what Moses may have said and done to encourage the Israelites. (Lesson 3)
- Explain what it means to be a "holy nation" and identify the responsibilities associated with this title. (Lesson 4)

Materials Needed Lesson 1—large sheet of paper; Lessons 1, 3, and 4—written directions for group work; Lesson 2—questions for group work.

The Tech Connection Refer to the general suggestions on page 7. The following are additional ideas for your Web page or Wikispace about Moses:
- Write an interview with Moses—What would Moses tell us today? What would he be proud of when looking at today's Jewish community? What might he be upset about?
- Set up a timeline. Add to the timeline after the class studies each chapter.
- Upload maps of where Moses lived and traveled.
- Upload artwork depicting events in this chapter. Students can write about what they learn from the art.
- Upload or establish links to songs, such as "Let My People Go," related to the Exodus.
- Research, write about, and upload pictures of the life of a shepherd or life in the palace of a pharaoh.
- Set up a glossary. Include, for example, *Covenant*, *judge*, *priest*, and *prophet*.
- Document examples of compassion and justice in our lives today. Upload photos of students engaged in acts of kindness.

Chapter 2 • Lesson 1

Essential Question: What are the qualities of a good leader?

Getting Started: (10 minutes) Students imagine they need to hire a shepherd. Students work with a partner to create a list of qualities they would include in a Help Wanted ad. Pairs share their suggestions with the class. Record the qualities on a large sheet of paper. Save the list for use in Lesson 2. Students identify qualities that are also those of a good leader. Inform students that Moses, and other leaders of ancient Israel, started as shepherds.

Exploring the Text:

1. (5 minutes) Explain that this chapter introduces Moses three different ways: in an artist's rendering, a biblical text, and a list of background information. Divide the class into three groups. Give the groups written directions as follows:

    ### Group A

    i   Read about Moses, the shepherd, in the **text based on Exodus 3–4** on page 8.

    ii As a group, respond to the following questions: What does God want? What might Moses want? What does Moses fear? What do you learn about Moses as a leader from this text?

    iii Retell Exodus 3–4 to the class and report your responses to the questions.

    ### Group B

    i   Look at the artist's **depiction of Moses** on page 8.

    ii As a group, respond to the following questions: What do you see in the picture? How does the artist portray Moses? What might have inspired the artist to paint Moses? What is the artist saying about Moses as a leader?

    iii Describe the portrait to the class and report your responses to the questions.

    ### Group C

    i   Read the **Prophet's Profile: Moses** on page 9.

    ii As a group, choose five pieces of information that help you understand Moses as a leader. Discuss why you have chosen these items and what you learn about Moses's leadership from each one.

    iii Tell the class which items you have chosen, why you have chosen them, and what you have learned about Moses as a leader from each one.

2. (10 minutes) Groups complete their first two tasks.

3. (15 minutes) Groups present their lenses on Moses as a leader. As they watch and listen to the presentations, ask students to write down one new idea they learn from each of the other groups. Students ask the other groups questions about their presentations. Students share new ideas they learned from the other groups.

Wrapping It Up: (5 minutes) Ask students to explain how we gain deeper understanding when we have different points of view. Discuss how life experiences, such as being brought up in the palace and then being a shepherd, might have helped Moses be a successful leader.

Chapter 2 • Lesson 2

Essential Question: How do the forces of justice and compassion guide us?

Getting Started: (5 minutes) Refer to the list of leadership qualities students brainstormed at the start of Lesson 1. Ask students to surmise which quality they think was most important to God when God chose Moses to lead the Jewish people.

Exploring the Text:

1. (5 minutes) Explain that the rabbis answered this question in a midrash. Clarify that a midrash, by supplying additional information, often answers questions we have that are not answered in the text of the Torah. Students read silently **Exodus Rabbah 2:2** (page 10) to discover why, according to the rabbis, God chose Moses. Students circle the reason given in the midrash. Ask: What does it mean to show compassion?

2. (10 minutes) Students read **Moses Discovers the Force of Justice and Compassion** (page 10) with a partner. Partners write 3–5 sentences in the voice of Moses explaining why he chose to accept God's command to lead the Israelites to freedom. Volunteers role-play being Moses and explain his acceptance of God's command.

3. (5 minutes) Students read silently the caption describing Miriam's cup (page 10). Students describe how Miriam's cup reminds us of God's compassion.

4. (5 minutes) Students read silently **Models of Compassion** (page 11) and underline the women who were responsible for saving Moses's life. *(Shifrah, Puah, Moses's mother, Moses's sister, and Pharaoh's daughter)*

5. (10 minutes) Divide the class into four groups: the midwives, Moses's mother, his sister, and Pharaoh's daughter. Be sure that the boys are comfortable playing girls' roles. Give everyone the following questions to answer as if they were that person: Why did you act to save the baby? What were the risks? What were the rewards? How did you feel knowing that Moses's survival was also dependent upon the compassion of others and that you alone would not be able to save him? Two students from the midwives group come to the front of the room, one to role-play Shifrah (or Puah) and one to interview her. Continue by having interviews with Moses's mother and sister, and Pharaoh's daughter.

6. (5 minutes) Students reflect on and write a response about the lessons the rabbis wanted to teach through their midrash on God naming Pharaoh's daughter Bityah (page 11). Students share their responses with a partner.

7. (5 minutes) Partners read **Sticky Stuff** (page 11) together. Students individually write their responses.

Wrapping It Up: (5 minutes) Volunteers describe their personal experiences that were shaped by acts of compassion. Ask: How does being compassionate make us better people? Why is being compassionate an essential quality of a good leader?

Chapter 2 • Lesson 3

Essential Question: What does it mean to be free?

Getting Started: (2–3 minutes) Students brainstorm a list of reasons they sing. Tell students that the first thing the Israelites did after crossing the Sea of Reeds was sing.

Exploring the Text:

1. (5 minutes) Sing Mi Chamochah as a class. Identify that this is sung daily before the Amidah in the morning and evening prayer services. Students read silently **Prayer Connection: Who Is Like God?** (page 12). Ask: How did the Israelites feel as they sang these words? What beliefs about God did they express? Why do you think we still sing this today?

2. (5 minutes) Ask students to listen to "Let My People Go," another song related to the Exodus, and to think of the emotions expressed in it. Play a recording, such as Louis Armstrong's version, which is available on the Internet. Students view the **art** on page 12 and discuss how the Exodus inspired others to resist oppression.

3. (5 minutes) Partners read **A Symbol of Freedom** (page 13). Partners discuss and write responses to the questions. Students share their thoughts on the motto. Ask: How is Benjamin Franklin's motto exemplified by Moses confronting Pharaoh?

4. (15 minutes) Divide the class into groups of 3–4 students. Give everyone written directions as follows: (i) Imagine you are Israelites, just freed from slavery, and walking through the desert. (ii) Record the joys and problems you may encounter, how you might feel, and what you may say or do as a reaction to these events. (iii) List some of the challenges and the rewards of being free. (iv) Read the opening of **A Prophet's Work Is Never Done** (page 12). (v) Compare this reading to your group's list.

5. (2–3 minutes) Discuss why it was difficult for the Israelites to maintain faith in God.

6. (10 minutes) Students read silently the **account based on Exodus 15, 16, and 17** (page 14) and locate Elim and the Wilderness of Sin on the **map** (page 13). Four students (a narrator, two Israelites, and Moses) act out the account. Ask the class: Why are the Israelites upset? Why do you think they blame Moses? How was Moses able to continue to lead the people with compassion? How do you keep your faith and commitment to a goal even when the challenges are great?

7. (5 minutes) Students read silently about Moses **establishing a judicial system** (pages 14–15). Ask: Why do we need a judicial system to live as free people? What do you learn about Moses as a leader from his establishment of this system? Students individually read and write responses to **What Do You Think?** (page 15).

Wrapping It Up: (5 minutes) Students imagine they are Moses. Students suggest words of encouragement Moses could say to the Israelites, just freed from slavery, to help them maintain their faith in God as they walk through the desert.

Chapter 2 • Lesson 4

Essential Question: What does it mean that we are a holy nation?

Getting Started: (2–3 minutes) Write on the board: A kingdom of priests. Students discuss the meaning of this phrase. Guide students to understand that it describes a nation in which each person is viewed as holy (has a divine quality) and lives a life guided by godliness. Briefly discuss students' interpretation of "godliness." (*performing mitzvot, acts of kindness and justice, being created in God's image*)

Exploring the Text:

1. (10 minutes) Write on the board: Why was it important that all Israelites experienced the giving of the commandments? Why are we required each Passover to imagine that we ourselves were slaves and witnesses at Mount Sinai? Partners read **A Radical Idea Becomes a People's Reason for Being** (pages 15–16) and write a brief response to the questions posted on the board. Students share their writings.

2. (5 minutes) Students read silently the first paragraph **based on Exodus 19:4–8** (page 16). Volunteers draw on the board their image of a nation transported on eagles' wings. Ask: What is a treasured possession of yours? How do you take care of a treasured possession? Students find the phrase "a kingdom of priests" and create a list of responsibilities for the Israelites as a kingdom of priests. Students read silently the second paragraph and then chorally read "Everything that Adonai has spoken we will do." Ask: How might it have felt to say this phrase together as an entire nation?

3. (10 minutes) Divide the class into three groups. Give everyone the following directions: (i) Read **The Teachings** (page 17). (ii) Explain how the laws given to the Israelites were different from the laws of their neighbors. (iii) Describe the terms of the Covenant. (What would God and the Israelites each do?) (iv) Give an example of an act of kindness, truth, or justice. Groups share their work.

4. (10 minutes) Assign each group one of the teachings from **Lessons of Justice and Compassion** (page 18). Groups take turns presenting to the class an explanation of their law and why this law is still important today. If time allows, groups may act out an example of a case related to this law.

5. (3 minutes) Volunteer reads the caption under the **photograph of the child** (page 18). Students reflect on why we are obligated to act with compassion but not obligated to *feel* compassionate.

6. (5 minutes) Partners read **In the Footsteps of the Prophets: Helen Suzman** (page 19). Students individually write how Suzman's role was similar to and different from Moses's. Partners share answers with one another.

Wrapping It Up: (5 minutes) Students discuss how they see themselves as members of a holy nation. Students reflect on what this means to them as they are about to become a bar or bat mitzvah.

Chapter 3
Samuel: Reluctant Kingmaker

Chapter Overview Longing for a child, Hannah vows that if she has one, that child will serve Adonai. In fulfillment of her vow, Hannah brings her son, Samuel, to Eli, the priest at the temple in Shiloh. At that time, the Israelites had a loose union of twelve tribes, each ruled by its own chieftain. Threatened by stronger, surrounding nations, the Israelites want to form a unified kingdom, ruled by a human king. Samuel, believing that only God can be King, tries to dissuade the Israelites and warns them of the potential dangers of being ruled by a single person. Ultimately, Samuel anoints Saul and then David to rule. David builds a strong united kingdom. Problems arise, however, under the reign of his son, Solomon, and the kingdom splits and weakens.

Core Concepts

- Being able to trust makes us stronger.
- It is important to uphold our core values while adapting to changes in society.
- Perseverance can enable us to overcome great challenges.
- Governments need a balance of power to best protect their citizens.

Learning Objectives Students will be able to:

- Describe Samuel's early years, his faith in God, and what they can learn about faith and trust from Samuel's example. (Lesson 1)
- Explain why the Israelites wanted a king, why Samuel objected to this, and what this account teaches about the challenge of upholding our values while adapting to changes in society. (Lesson 2)
- Recount the events between the Philistines and the Israelites, and reflect on how these tensions heightened the Israelites' desire for a king. (Lesson 3)
- Outline the rise and fall of the Israelite kingdom; define the roles of king, priest, and prophet; and suggest how they can apply an idea learned from Yitzḥak Rabin or Samuel to their own lives. (Lesson 4)

Materials Needed Lesson 2—sheet of paper with the outline of six 3" x 3" squares for each student; Lesson 4—copy of grid for each student to chart the successes and failure of the early Israelite kingdom.

The Tech Connection Refer to the general suggestions on page 7. The following are additional ideas for your Web page or Wikispace about Samuel:

- Add the events of this chapter to the timeline started while studying chapter 2.
- Add definitions for words such as *anoint* and *chieftain* to the glossary.
- Upload maps from the time of Samuel through the division of the kingdoms. Identify places mentioned in this chapter, such as Eben-ezer and Ashdod.
- Scan and upload cartoons students created about Deborah. (Lesson 2)
- Research and write about bronze and iron weapons in antiquity. Post pictures of weapons.
- Upload and critique images of artwork that depict the events of this chapter, such as the god Dagon on the floor or Samuel anointing a king.
- Research and write about King David as a musician and author of the Psalms.

Chapter 3 • Lesson 1

Essential Question: How does having trust, in people or in God, help us in our everyday lives?

Getting Started: (5 minutes) Students tell of personal experiences when someone has earned their trust and how this has influenced what they will do for the person.

Exploring the Text:

1. (10 minutes) Three students—playing a narrator, Eli, and Samuel—come to the front of the room and present the **text based on Samuel 1:9–3:10** (page 20). As a class, students compare the early lives of Moses and Samuel *(unusual births and upbringing)* and their calls to prophecy. Ask: Why did Eli, but not Samuel, realize it was God calling? How do you think Samuel felt when he was told God was calling him? How does this account demonstrate trust and faith in people and in God? Why was it important that Eli and Samuel both had this faith and trust?

2. (15 minutes) Students read the items listed in **Prophet's Profile: Samuel** (page 21) with a partner. A volunteer comes to the front of the room to act out one of the items. Classmates guess which item is being presented. The student who guesses the correct item and tells one thing we learn from this item comes to the front to act out another item. Continue until each item has been acted out and discussed. Guide students to derive insights, such as the following, from this list:

   - Samuel lived over 3,000 years ago.
   - His mother had great faith in God and believed that God heard her.
   - He was from the tribe of Ephraim and, therefore, was not a priest (priests, Kohanim, are descendants of Aaron from the tribe of Levi).
   - Samuel moved away from his family as a toddler and served God.
   - He lived at a major turning point in our history, when the Israelites changed from small self-governing tribes to a stronger united nation.
   - He anointed the first two kings of Israel even though he was against having a human king.
   - He taught the Israelites, including the kings, to honor and serve God.

3. (5 minutes) Students speculate about why Samuel anointed Saul and David despite his opposition to having a human king. Ask: How might his faith in God have helped Samuel when he anointed the first kings of Israel?

4. (5 minutes) Students read and discuss the **Prayer Connection: Stand Up and Speak Silently from Your Heart** (page 22) with a partner. Have students describe the photograph of the girl praying. Call on volunteers to share their responses to the questions in the caption.

Wrapping It Up: (5 minutes) Students discuss how having faith and trust influenced Samuel, Eli, and Hannah. Students reflect on what they learn from the actions of these great biblical figures.

Chapter 3 • Lesson 2

Essential Question: How do we maintain our values as we undergo changes in our lives?

Getting Started: (5 minutes) Ask: Have you ever formed or joined a club, team, or group? Why did you become part of this group? What were the benefits? What were the challenges? What rules did you have to follow? Were you comfortable with all the rules? What would you do if there were rules you objected to?

Exploring the Text:

1. (5 minutes) Tell students they are about to study how the Israelites formed a new "group," going from a loose union of tribes to a united kingdom. Students look at the **map** (page 24) and locate Samuel's tribal land, Ephraim. Students read silently the three paragraphs of **Samuel—Prophet, Priest, and Judge** (page 22). As a class, students describe the military situation for the tribes and the different roles of the chieftain, priest, and prophet.

2. (10 minutes) Give each student a sheet of paper with six blank squares (see Materials on page 16). Partners read **Deborah of Lappidot** (page 23). Each student creates a four-to-six cell cartoon illustrating the events of Judges 4:4–5. Students record their responses to the questions at the end of the passage. Volunteers show their cartoons to classmates and share their responses to the questions.

3. (5 minutes) Partners finish reading **Samuel—Prophet, Priest, and Judge** (page 24) and underline Samuel's reasons for not having a king.

4. (5 minutes) Students describe the **art depicting Ramses, Horus, and Anubis** (page 25) and suggest what the artist believed about the pharaohs and gods. Students individually read and write responses to **The Tradition of God-Kings.** (page 25) Volunteers share their answers with the class. Ask: What values would be threatened if the Israelites were commanded to believe that their leader was God?

5. (15 minutes) Divide class into two groups: (A) Israelites for a united kingdom (B) God is our Ruler. Each group prepares a short persuasive speech supporting their cause. A representative from each group presents the speech to the class. After both sides have been presented, students share their personal views as to the pros and cons of the Israelites being ruled by a human king.

6. (5 minutes) Partners read, discuss, and write their responses to **What Do You Think?** (page 25) and **To Change or Not to Change? That Is the Question** (page 26).

Wrapping It Up: (5 minutes) Ask: How could the Israelites protect their ability to uphold their beliefs and values while under the dominion of a human king? How does living in a democratic society affect our ability to uphold our beliefs and values?

Chapter 3 • Lesson 3

Essential Question: Why do we continue to try even when the odds seem to be against us?

Getting Started: (5 minutes) Students tell of situations during which they felt their chances of success were slim, yet they continued to work toward their goal and eventually succeeded. Students share why and how they sustained their efforts.

Exploring the Text:

1. (10 minutes) Students read silently the first four paragraphs of **The Menace of the Philistines** (page 26). Students express how, as Israelites, they may have felt about having a king. Students identify what the Philistines and the Israelites each brought to the battlefield to defeat the enemy. Students read about the **Philistine's weapons and the Israelites' Ark** (page 27). Students suggest why it wasn't enough to bring the Ark of the Covenant and recommend what else the Israelites needed to do to be successful. Discuss how this text reminds us that we are partners with God; we can turn to God as a source of strength and guidance but must act to achieve our goals.

2. (10 minutes) Partners finish reading **The Menace of the Philistines** (pages 26–27). They imagine they are Philistines and write an eyewitness report of what happened after they captured the Ark. Volunteers take turns reporting their experiences in Ashdod to the class.

3. (10 minutes) Students read silently the first paragraph of **Samuel Defeats the Philistines** (page 27). Lead a discussion based on the three questions in bold at the bottom of the page. Students share why they do or do not sympathize with the Israelites who lost faith. Discuss how it can be challenging to maintain faith when you are struggling.

4. (10 minutes) Students work in groups of 3–4. Groups read the text inspired by **1 Samuel 7:2–4** (page 28) and imagine that they are musicians who have been commissioned to compose background music for a stage production about Samuel. Assign each group one section of the text. Each group discusses and then lists the instruments and types of music that would fit each sentence or paragraph of their assigned section. A volunteer reads the account line by line, pausing for a group representative to describe or simulate the music that would suit the event. Students discuss why and how the music changed from one group to the next.

5. (5 minutes) Read aloud the closing paragraph of **Samuel Defeats the Philistines** (page 28). Students predict what the Israelites will do next, now that they have defeated the Philistines.

Wrapping It Up: (5 minutes) Students give examples and explain how something Samuel did or said can inspire us to persevere when we are in a challenging situation.

Chapter 3 • Lesson 4

Essential Question: What does leadership look like?

Getting Started: (5 minutes) Students give examples of a person or group having too much power. Students suggest possible ramifications of this imbalance of power.

Exploring the Text:

1. (10 minutes) Students offer reasons why the Israelites should have recognized the disadvantages of being ruled by a king. *(They were slaves in Egypt; they were living among nations ruled by kings.)* Students read silently **"Give Us a King"** (pages 28–29). Several volunteers come to the board; each illustrates one of the situations described by Samuel, such as sons running before the king's chariot. Students refer to the illustrations to review each situation and reflect on the problematic aspects of that situation. Students suggest why Samuel was compelled to warn the Israelites about the dangers of having a king.

2. (10 minutes) Four volunteers take the parts of narrator, Adonai, Samuel, and Saul, and act out the events from **1 Samuel 9:15–16, 10:1, 10:6** (page 30). Students respond to questions such as: What is God's charge to Samuel? What qualities will make Saul a good leader? What is the meaning of "the spirit of God entered Saul"? Students describe the **art depicting Samuel and Saul** (page 30). Students interpret what the artist was saying about these two leaders.

3. (5 minutes) Students read silently **The Conscience of the King and the People** (page 31). Ask: Who would you rather be—the king, a priest, or a prophet? Why? What responsibilities would you need to fulfill? What were the benefits of having three different leaders?

4. (10 minutes) Before class, prepare and copy a chart made up of four columns and five rows. Label the columns: king; strengths and successes; weaknesses and failures; status of the kingdom. In the left hand column, label the rows: Saul; David; Solomon; post-Solomon. Give everyone a copy of the chart. Individually or with a partner students read **Historical Note: The Kingdom Unites then Cracks** (page 31) and complete the chart. As a class, students discuss the rise and fall of the Israelite kingdom. Students focus on causes of problems that began under Solomon and speculate how a balance of power might have prevented problems.

5. (10 minutes) Students individually complete **Let's Make a Midrash** (page 32) and share their midrash with a neighbor.

Wrapping It Up: (10 minutes) Remind students that the modern State of Israel is an example of a government that has a balance of power and that the prime minister is Israel's top government official. Students independently read and write responses to the questions from **In the Footsteps of the Prophets: Yitzḥak Rabin** (page 33). Students share responses in a full class discussion. Students name one idea they learned from Samuel that they can apply to their own lives.

Chapter 4
Elijah: Zealous Critic of the King

Chapter Overview The bible includes little information on Elijah's personal history. Biblical, rabbinic, and folklore accounts combine to present a complex portrait of Elijah—at times stern, at other times almost playful. According to tradition, Elijah never died—he was taken up to heaven in a fiery chariot. The stories of Elijah portray a prophet who was passionately loyal to God and the people of Israel, a man who spoke out against injustice and faithlessness. Elijah challenged the evil King Ahab and Queen Jezebel of Israel who worshipped foreign idols and who murdered innocent people. A model of a person who will fight for justice, Elijah has come to represent our hope for a better world.

Core Concepts

- Historical events and traditional stories direct our moral compass.
- Faith, commitment, and courage are essential for us to live according to our beliefs.
- Jewish rituals awaken our consciences, reminding us to pursue justice and truth.
- Jewish traditions and values teach that it is our responsibility to build a better world.

Learning Objectives Students will be able to:

- Derive a moral lesson based on an account or information about Elijah. (Lesson 1)
- Retell a story about Elijah and explain how it demonstrates the importance of faith, commitment, and courage. (Lesson 2)
- Identify ways that they, like Elijah, might hear and respond to the voice of godliness. (Lesson 3)
- Describe what they can do—even if it means challenging a respected authority figure—to fight against injustice. (Lesson 4)

Materials Needed Lesson 1—supplies for self-portrait; Lesson 2—One question sheet per student; Lesson 3—one question sheet per student; Lesson 4—poster board of Elijah's cup (to prepare poster board, fill the board with an outline of a large goblet. Write the heading "In Pursuit of Justice, We Can Overcome…" at the top of the board, and "Elijah's Cup" at the bottom of the goblet), three 2" x 3" pieces of light colored paper per student, glue stick.

The Tech Connection Refer to the general suggestions on page 7. The following are additional ideas for your Web page or Wikispace about Elijah:

- Upload links to video recordings of the song "Eliyahu Hanavi."
- Scan and upload students' self-portraits. (Lesson 1)
- Post students' writings and illustrations about their hopes and what they can do to fight injustice. (Lesson 4)
- Add to glossary. Include higher level vocabulary words, such as *vagrant* and *zealous*.
- Locate and scan the pages from Moby Dick in which Elijah appears.
- Document examples of compassion and justice in our lives today. Upload photos of students engaged in acts of kindness.
- Upload references to "social justice" from current newspapers and periodicals.
- Research and report on the life and contributions of Bella Abzug.

Chapter 4 • Lesson 1

Essential Question: How do both historical events and traditional stories direct our moral compass?

Getting Started: (10 minutes) Students recount stories and legends they have heard and historical events they have studied that have a moral lesson. Explain that there are numerous accounts about Elijah. These accounts, whether historical or legendary, reflect Jewish values and beliefs, and help guide us morally.

Exploring the Text:

1. (5 minutes) Refer to the chapter title and explain the meaning of "zealous" (passionately devoted to a purpose). Students read the account of **Sandalphon coming to earth as Elijah** (page 34). Students write two things about Elijah and one moral they have learned from this legend. Students share what they have learned and discuss their general first impressions of Elijah.

2. (10 minutes) Partners read **Prophet's Profile: Elijah** (page 35) and number the three items they find most interesting. Students share their lists and explain why they chose these items. Students suggest one or more moral lessons derived from Elijah's profile.

3. (5 minutes) Students individually read **The Man and the Mystery** (page 36). In a class discussion, guide students to understand that Elijah can inspire us even though there is much we do not know about him. Students suggest ways "passionate loyalty to God and to the people of Israel" might be demonstrated.

4. (10 minutes) Students read **Will the Real Elijah Please Stand Up?** (page 36). Ask students where Elijah features in the Passover seder tradition. (*we open the door for him*) Students consider the descriptions of Elijah on page 36, and role-play Elijah entering the door to their home and speaking with their family. Lead, or teach the students to sing, *Eliyahu Hanavi*. Discuss the mood of the song.

5. (10 minutes) Groups of 3–4 students look at the **art depicting Elijah going up to heaven** (page 36) and write what it tells them about Elijah. Using a Bible or the Internet, groups read 2 Kings 2:1–12. Groups write and share new items they learn about Elijah from this passage. Discuss how this text sheds light on the art.

6. (20 minutes) Partners discuss the question in the **photo caption** (page 37). Students individually read and complete **What Color Is the Real You?** (page 37). Class brainstorms other traits, and students suggest colors that express those traits. Students create individual abstract self-portraits, incorporating the colors they feel describe themselves. Suggested media include watercolors, torn paper, colored pencils and/or crayons. Display the portraits.

Wrapping It Up: (5 minutes) Partners reflect on today's class and identify two Jewish beliefs or values embedded in the lesson. Students share their answers.

Chapter 4 • Lesson 2

***Essential Question:* Why does it take courage to live according to our beliefs?**

Getting Started: (5 minutes) Students identify personality traits and qualities that are essential if we are to live according to our beliefs. Explain that in this lesson, students will reflect on traits and qualities of Elijah that helped him to follow his beliefs.

Exploring the Text:

1. (5 minutes) A volunteer reads the caption describing the **map of the divided kingdom** (page 38). To deepen students' understanding of the political, social, and religious situation, ask questions such as: When did the kingdom divide? *(after Solomon's death)* Did Elijah live in the northern or the southern kingdom? *(northern)* In which kingdom was the Holy Temple located? *(southern)* What religious problems might have arisen in the north? *(needed a place to do sacrifices)*

2. (10 minutes) Assign students (individually, pairs, or small groups) one of the following characters: God, Elijah, Ahab, Jezebel, Israelites, Prophets of Baal and Asherah. Give everyone a page with these questions: *What does your character want? Why does your character want this? What do you think your character will do to get this?* Students read **The Wicked King and the "Troublemaker of Israel"** (page 38) and write responses to the three questions. Students share their responses.

3. (10 minutes) Divide the class into three groups: Elijah, Israelites, Prophets of Baal. Groups read the **account based on 1 Kings 18:21–39** (page 39) and prepare a retelling of the events from the point of view of their character. A representative of each group presents its version. Students share what they learned about faith and courage from this account.

4. (5 minutes) Lead class in chorally repeating *Adonai Hu ha'Elohim* seven times. Students suggest why we repeat this seven times at the close of Yom Kippur. Students individually read **Prayer Connection: Yom Kippur Declaration** (page 40). The class shares responses to the questions in the second paragraph.

5. (10 minutes) Partners read the top paragraph of page 40 and the first five paragraphs of **A Still, Small Voice** and list how the events described on pages 38–40 strengthened or weakened the faith of Jezebel and of Elijah. Students share their lists. A volunteer role-plays Elijah and explains why he now has the courage to come out of the cave and face Ahab and Jezebel.

Wrapping It Up: (5 minutes) Write on the board: Identify something you believe in and describe how you sometimes need courage to follow this belief. Students individually write responses.

Chapter 4 • Lesson 3

***Essential Question:** What is the relationship between listening to our conscience and being a great leader?*

Getting Started: (5 minutes) Students describe situations in which they spoke up against something they believe is wrong, explain why they spoke up, and tell how it felt to voice an unpopular opinion. Tell students that in today's lesson they will read about Elijah speaking up against the king of Israel.

Exploring the Text:

1. (10 minutes) Partners read the first two paragraphs on page 41 and write their own definitions for "the voice of godliness" and "spiritual amps." and The class designs a single definition for each term. (*something that reminds us to listen to our conscience; Jewish laws and values that guide us to pursue justice.*) Consider how rituals, such as **hearing the shofar** (photo on page 41), can help us listen to our conscience. Students identify additional rituals and suggest how they can serve as "spiritual amps." Students respond to the closing question in paragraph 2.

2. (10 minutes) Partners read **Where Is God?** (page 41), individually write responses to the questions, and read their writings to one another. Students share their thoughts as a class. Students discuss whether it is hard or easy for them to sense God. Discuss how and why performing mitzvot, such as being just or merciful, may or may not lead someone to feel God in his or her life.

3. (10 minutes) Review how Jezebel wanted Elijah dead, and that fearing for his life, Elijah fled to the wilderness. In small groups, students read **It's Not Just Unfair—It's Murder!** (pages 41–42), including the **account based on 1 Kings 21:1–23**.

    Give everyone the following questions to complete with their group: (i) *How did Ahab and Jezebel break each of the four commandments recorded on the bottom of page 42? (ii) How might Ahab have felt when he heard Elijah's words? (iii) What did Elijah risk by speaking up? (iv) What might have happened if Elijah did not speak up? (v) How do you think Elijah found the courage to speak up?*

4. (5 minutes) Students individually read and complete **Follow Me** (page 43). Students meet with a partner and share their responses to the questions about leadership traits.

5. (5 minutes) A volunteer reads the caption for the **photo of the infant** (page 43). Students respond to the caption questions, debate if leaders are made or born, and suggest an important lesson that would help someone become a strong leader.

Wrapping It Up: (10 minutes) Ask: Do you think Elijah was born or made a leader? How did encountering God help make Elijah a stronger leader? What can we learn about how to be a good leader from Elijah?

Chapter 4 • Lesson 4

***Essential Question:** What do Jewish traditions and values teach us about our responsibility to build a better world?*

Getting Started: (5 minutes) Students describe situations in which they were told to mind their own business. Students discuss the difference between meddling in someone else's affairs and speaking out to correct an injustice. Students identify qualities of an unjust situation. (*examples: the weak and disenfranchised suffer, there's a wide gap between the haves and have-nots, people take advantage of others, innocents get hurt*)

Exploring the Text:

1. (5 minutes) Students read silently the first two paragraphs of **A Meddler or a Mensch?** (page 44). Students give examples, from history or from today, of people, like Elijah, who spoke up in pursuit of justice. In a discussion, guide students to appreciate that while speaking up against injustice is a universal value, Elijah's words and actions teach us that it is a specific Jewish value.

2. (10 minutes) A volunteer reads aloud the caption for the **photograph of the baseball team** (page 44). The class shares responses to the questions in the caption. Divide the class into groups of 3–4 students. Each group creates, and then presents, a scenario in which one of them disagrees with an authority figure. As a reminder of what to include, write on the board: What is the disagreement about? What does each person think? How can you resolve the disagreement in a polite, respectful manner?

3. (5 minutes) Partners finish reading **A Meddler or a Mensch?** (page 44). Partners write one way they can make a difference in their home, in their classroom, as part of a team, and in the synagogue. Students share their lists with the class.

4. (10 minutes) Read aloud the caption for the **photograph of Elijah's cup** (page 44). Give each student three small pieces of paper. On the first, students write one injustice they hope will be overcome. Collect the papers and read them aloud as you mount them on the background of the Elijah's cup poster (see Materials on page 21). Students write, on a second paper, what they can do individually to overcome an injustice and, on a third paper, what they can do as part of a group. Collect and mount these papers inside Elijah's cup. Display the Elijah's cup poster on a bulletin board.

5. (10 minutes) Students meet again as a group, read **In the Footsteps of the Prophets: Bella Abzug** (page 45), discuss the questions, and then record their answers. Students share their answers with the class.

Wrapping It Up: (10 minutes). Students return to page 37 and discuss the issues raised in **What Color Is the Real You?**: What might you want to ask Elijah about how to handle fear or self-doubt? Who in today's world or in your personal life reminds you of Elijah and why?

Chapter 5
Amos: Faithful Friend of the Covenant

Chapter Overview Little is known about Amos's personal life, but it is believed that he lived a simple, modest life as a shepherd in the southern kingdom of Judah. Around 750 BCE, Amos began to prophecy to the wealthy citizens in the cities of the northern kingdom of Israel. He warned them that if they did not repent and honor God's covenant they would be destroyed. Although the Israelites did not heed Amos's words, the prophecies of Amos continue to remind us of the Jewish commitment to pursue justice and to work toward building a better world.

Core Concepts

- It often takes courage to speak up for social justice.
- We are obligated to try to influence others to live ethically.
- Jewish values can guide us as we adapt to an ever-changing world.

Learning Objectives Students will be able to:

- Give examples of how Amos inspires us to speak up against popular opinion in pursuit of justice. (Lesson 1)
- Discuss how Amos's actions and words teach us to speak up in hopes of convincing others to change their ways and live more ethically. (Lesson 2)
- Provide examples of how traditional Jewish values guide us to live ethically as we adapt to our ever-changing world. (Lesson 3)

Materials Needed Lesson 1—one sheet of lined paper per student; Lesson 2—chart for outlining Amos 1:1–2:4; Lesson 3—(optional) a video or audio recording of "The Times They Are A-Changin'."

The Tech Connection Refer to the general suggestions on page 7. The following are additional ideas for your Web page or Wikispace about Amos:

- Upload links to video recordings of the song "The Times They Are A-Changin'."
- Students post information about rallies and letter writing campaigns that oppose social injustices.
- Post students' reflections on: When and how do you think people find the courage to speak out against popular opinion? (Lesson 1)
- Students choose a quote from Amos and create an artistic expression of the quote. Upload the art, music, or video of a dance created by the students. (Lesson 2)
- Record videos in class of students role-playing Amos or Judge Ginsburg. (Lesson 3) Upload the videos to the Web.
- Students use the Internet to research—and then report on—King Uzziah of Judah and King Jeroboam II of Israel.
- Using the Internet, students learn to chant one or two verses from Amos. Students record themselves chanting the Hebrew followed by an English translation.
- Students research sycamore trees and their fruits, and post images and information on the Web.
- Students research and report on the life and contributions of Judge Ginsburg.

Chapter 5 • Lesson 1

Essential Question: What gives us the courage to speak up for social justice, even when our opinion is unpopular?

Getting Started: (3 minutes) Students cite examples of how Moses, Samuel, and Elijah, listening to their moral consciences, spoke up against popular opinion and/or an authority figure. Tell students that Amos, like these other prophets, had to speak out against the majority.

Exploring the Text:

1. (10 minutes) Partners read the **account inspired by Amos 3:7–8; 7:14-15** (page 46) and list similarities between Amos and Moses. *(shepherds, in the wilderness, hear the Voice, hesitant to speak)* Partners share their lists with the class. Students suggest why, according to tradition, God chose people with these qualities to be prophets. Ask: If you were choosing someone to fight for a cause you believe in, what qualities would you look for in that person?

2. (5 minutes) Students read silently **Prophet's Profile: Amos** (page 47) and examine the **map of Amos's travels** (page 51). To deepen students' understanding of Amos, ask questions such as: Why do you think Amos's name is fitting for him? What was a major religious problem for the people living in the northern kingdom of Israel? If Amos was from Tekoa, near the wilderness, how well would he be able to relate to city people?

3. (7 minutes) A volunteer reads the caption next to the **art representing Amos** (page 48). Divide the class into groups of 3–5 students. Each group discusses and then records its responses to the three questions included in the caption. A representative from each group shares its responses with the class. Students name past and present leaders and note if they were, or were not, raised in politically or socially powerful families. Students suggest why being raised in a powerful family is not a prerequisite for becoming a persuasive leader.

4. (10 minutes) Students read silently **Who Can Ignore the Roar of the Lion?** (pages 48–49). The class discusses the questions in the closing paragraphs.

5. (15 minutes) Students meet again in groups. Each group creates and presents a short skit, or role-play, in which a person has to speak up against popular opinion in pursuit of justice. After the presentations, students discuss how they would feel in a similar situation.

Wrapping It Up: (5 minutes) Give each student a sheet of lined paper. Write on the board: When and how do you think people find the courage to speak out against popular opinion? Students individually write their responses to the question. If you have a Web page, post these writings.

Chapter 5 • Lesson 2

Essential Question: How do we convince others to live ethically?

Getting Started: (5 minutes) Volunteers tell what action they take when they see another person doing something wrong and they want that person to behave differently. Students suggest what it might have felt like to be Amos, a shepherd, as he entered the affluent streets of Bethel.

Exploring the Text:

1. (10 minutes) Before class, prepare and copy a chart made up of three columns and nine rows. Label the columns: Paragraph #, Israelites, Amos. Beginning with the second row, number the rows in the left-hand column: 1, 2, 3, 4, 5, 6, 7, Amos 2:4–7, 12. Title the chart: What were they thinking and feeling? Give everyone a copy of the chart. You may also choose to draw a similar chart on the board for recording ideas shared when the class reviews their charts.

    Partners read **Amos Prophesies at the Temple in Bethel**, including the **account inspired by Amos 1:1–2:4** (pages 49–50). Partners then discuss and write in the chart what they imagine the citizens of Bethel and Amos were thinking and feeling based on each paragraph. As a class, students share their work and discuss what they've learned about the Israelites and Amos from their charts.

2. (5 minutes) Lead class in a dramatic choral reading of Amos's prophecy from **Amos 2:4–7, 12** (page 50). Students suggest what the Israelites and Amos were thinking and feeling as Amos uttered these words. Record their suggestions in the last row of the chart.

3. (5 minutes) A volunteer reads the caption describing the **photo of the boy with goats** (page 51). Students share responses to the questions included in the caption. Volunteers role-play being Amos and an Israelite who advises him why he should or should not use technology to prophesy, or why he should prophesy only in person.

4. (10 minutes) Students read silently the first paragraph of **The Call to Honor the Covenant** (page 52). Students discuss what Amos wants, does, and says. Lead students in reading chorally **Amos 3:2, 5:6, 5:15, 5:24** (page 52). Volunteers interpret the meaning of "Let justice flow like water, righteousness like a mighty stream." A volunteer reads the caption next to the **photo** (page 52). Students individually choose another quote from Amos and describe to a partner how they might express it through art, dance, or music.

5. (5 minutes) Partners read **Prayer Connection: A Call for Forgiveness** (page 52), discuss their responses to the questions, and then record their responses. Volunteers share their responses with the class.

Wrapping It Up: (5 minutes) Ask: How can Amos's actions and words inspire us to challenge others to change their ways to live more ethically?

Chapter 5 • Lesson 3

Essential Question: How do Jewish values guide us as we adapt to our ever-changing world?

Getting Started: (5 minutes) Students brainstorm a list of Jewish values that are as important and relevant today as they were a hundred and even a thousand years ago. Tell students that in this lesson they will consider how Jewish values have guided us for thousands of years to adapt and respond with justice to an ever-changing world.

Exploring the Text:

1. (10 minutes) If possible, play a segment of a video or audio recording of "The Times They Are A-Changin'." Inform students that this song has been recorded by countless musicians and, like the words of the prophets, has stood the test of time. Divide the class into groups of 3–5 students. Groups read **The Times They Are A-Changin'** (page 53), discuss, and then record their responses to the questions. Students suggest how we maintain faith and continue to fight for a cause even when others don't seem to be listening or following our words.

2. (10 minutes) Students read silently **What Became of the People Israel** and **The Price of Corruption and Greed** (pages 54–55). Assign one or two questions from these paragraphs to small groups of students. Groups discuss their question(s), and a representative from each group shares its answers with the class. Students tell how they or family members have protested.

3. (10 minutes) Students read silently **Do the Right Thing** (page 54) and write responses to the questions. In small groups, students share their responses. Group members take turns telling about a time when they stepped out of their comfort zone. Students explain how and why they found the courage to do this, and how they would feel about doing this again.

4. (10 minutes) A student reads aloud the caption under the **photograph of the life preserver ring** (page 55). Students tell how they have helped others through small acts. Partners read **Must I Stand Up Alone?** (page 56). Students individually write and then share their responses with their partners Volunteers role-play giving advice to a friend who is reluctant to speak out. Students read silently the caption entitled **Poll Your Friends** (page 56). Consider having students search for favorite networking sites in class.

5. (5 minutes) Students read **In the Footsteps of the Prophets: Ruth Bader Ginsburg** (page 57). Students suggest which Jewish values influenced Judge Ginsburg. Students voice and then individually write responses to the questions.

Wrapping It Up: (5 minutes) Volunteers role-play being either Amos or Judge Ginsburg advising the class about when and why they should speak up, which injustices they should try to remedy, and how they should proceed.

Chapter 6
Isaiah: Righteous Spirit of Worship

Chapter Overview Most scholars agree that the Book of Isaiah was written by or about several different prophets. Many divide the book into three parts: First Isaiah, Chapters 1–39—740 to 688 BCE in Judah; Second Isaiah, Chapters 40–55—shortly after 586 BCE in Babylonia; Third Isaiah, Chapters 56–66—440 to 420 BCE in Jerusalem. Each prophet relayed a message specific to the historical and social circumstances of his time; collectively these prophets inspire us to speak out against immoral behavior, to be compassionate, to dream of a better future, and to give hope to others. Isaiah's vision of a better world is one in which all people worship God by showing compassion and pursuing justice and peace.

Core Concepts

- It is our responsibility to speak out against unethical behavior.
- Tradition guides us to show compassion when confronting someone for a wrongdoing.
- The Land of Israel has been in the hearts of the Jewish people for thousands of years.
- To build a better world, we need to have a vision and work toward that vision.

Learning Objectives Students will be able to:

- Identify factors that influence, and enhance, their readiness to speak up against wrongdoings. (Lesson 1)
- Explain the importance and benefits of being compassionate when confronting someone for a wrongdoing. (Lesson 2)
- Cite examples from the Bible, siddur, and history that demonstrate how the Land of Israel has been in the hearts of the Jewish people for thousands of years. (Lesson 3)
- Identify something good in their class, school, or synagogue, and describe how it could be better and what they can do to make it better. (Lesson 4)

Materials Needed Lesson 1— recording of "Lo Yisa Goy El Goy Ḥerev"; Lesson 2—Tanakh or Internet, large sheet of paper (optional), copies of a chart made of four columns (labeled: Isaiah, Chapters 1–39, Chapters 40–55, Chapters 56–66) and five rows (labeled: Isaiah (also column heading), Which Isaiah? Where did he preach? When did he preach? What was his message?); Lesson 4—sheet of blank paper for each student; lyrics to "Im Tirtzu"; one copy per student of "Vision Page" questions.

The Tech Connection Refer to the general suggestions on page 7. The following are additional ideas for your Web page or Wikispace about Isaiah:

- Upload links to video recordings of the song "Lo Yisa Goy El Goy Ḥerev."
- Research and write about the Assyrians, the conquest of the Northern Kingdom of Israel, and/or the fall of Judah.
- List the *Haftarot* of Consolation and when they are recited.
- Upload images of the first Holy Temple (Solomon's Temple).
- Students create or find online art images based on Isaiah's verses, such as "The wolf shall live with the lamb." Upload the art images along with the biblical verses.
- Begin a class project that will help make a "better world." Describe and track student activities related to this project. Upload photographs of students participating in the project.

Chapter 6 • Lesson 1

Essential Question: How should we respond to unethical behavior in our own community?

Getting Started: (5 minutes) Students recount experiences when they witnessed someone speaking out against unfair treatment of others in their school or community. Remind students not to include any names or circumstances that would embarrass others. Students express why they admire the speaker.

Exploring the Text:

1. (10 minutes) Ask students to stand and join with you as you recite *Kadosh, kadosh, kadosh Adonai Tz'va'ot, m'lo chol ha'aretz k'vodo* and rise on your toes at each *kadosh*. Students suggest why we rise three times. Students read **Prayer Connection: You're an Angel** (page 60) and compare their suggestions to that in the reading. Students read silently the **text based on Isaiah 1–6** (page 58). Ask questions about Isaiah's call to prophecy. Suggested questions include: How did Isaiah's neighbors treat one another? What does Isaiah envision? Why does the seraph brush a coal over Isaiah's lips? How do you think Isaiah felt when he heard the Voice? Why do you think he answered *Hineni*?

2. (10 minutes) Sing or play a recording of "Lo Yisa Goy El Goy Ḥerev." Students locate and circle the English meaning of this phrase in **Prophet's Profile: Isaiah** (page 59). Students discuss why we still sing these ancient verses. Volunteers take turns reading the items about Isaiah. After each item is read, students explain how this item gives us insight into Isaiah's role as a prophet. For example, the first item informs us that he was living near the Holy Temple.

3. (10 minutes) Divide the class into groups of 3–4 students. Groups read the beginning of **Jumping for Justice** (page 60). Group members share personal experiences about times when they were ready to speak up and times when they were not ready to do so. Groups compile two lists of situations: Quick to speak up; Hesitant to speak up. A representative from each group shares its list with the class. The class discusses what factors influence—and build—their readiness to speak up.

4. (5 minutes) Partners read the **text inspired by Isaiah 1, Proverbs 21:3** (pages 60–61). Partners identify and list six wrongdoings committed by the Israelites and then write a comparable wrongdoing of today. For example: An Israelite merchant selling watered-down wine is comparable to a vendor who sells knockoff watches. Students share their lists with the class. A volunteer reads Isaiah's words to the Israelites dramatically.

5. (5 minutes) Partners read **What Do You Think?** (page 61). Partners share and then record their responses.

Wrapping It Up: (5 minutes) Students role-play being Isaiah speaking out against some contemporary wrongdoings students listed as comparable to those of the Israelites.

Chapter 6 • Lesson 2

***Essential Question:** What is the connection between responding compassionately to wrongdoing and hoping for a better future?*

Getting Started: (5 minutes) Students suggest what they think is the most effective manner to respond to someone who has knowingly or unknowingly done something wrong. Explain that in this lesson, the class will look at what we learn from Isaiah about how to confront a "wrongdoer."

Exploring the Text:

1. (10 minutes) Partners find Leviticus (Vayikra) 19:17—in a Tanakh or on the Internet—and read the verse aloud in English and/or in Hebrew. Students read silently the first two paragraphs of **The Responsibility to Confront Wrongdoers** (page 62). Students compare the guidelines of Maimonides (1135–1204, who lived in Spain, Morocco, Israel, and Egypt) to their descriptions of how they think someone should be approached if they have done something wrong. Partners find and read aloud **Leviticus 19:18** (page 62). Students individually respond to the questions in this section. The class then shares their responses.

2. (10 minutes) Students give their own definitions of a religious Jew. Write their suggestions on the board. Students read silently the continuation of **Jumping for Justice** (page 62). As a class, students compare their ideas of a religious Jew to Isaiah's concept. The class shares their thoughts on how rituals help us appreciate our own lives and motivate us to help others.

3. (5 minutes) A volunteer reads the caption next to the **photo of the boy in the dog crate** (page 63). The class brainstorms ways to overcome the impulse to "put someone in the doghouse." Reinforce the idea that the photo is just a visual metaphor for this concept. Record the list on large paper and/or include the list on your Prophet's Web site.

4. (10 minutes) Students share what it feels like when they take responsibility for a mistake they have made. Guide students to understand that having mixed emotions, such as relief and embarrassment, is a natural part of owning up to a wrong. Partners read **We All Make Mistakes** (page 63). Partners discuss and then write how taking personal responsibility for a wrong can help us be more compassionate when confronting others. As a class, share responses to the questions in the caption next to the **photo of the woman comforting two boys** (page 63).

5. (10 minutes) Divide the class into small groups. Give everyone a copy of the Isaiah chart (see Materials Needed on page 30). Groups read **One, Two, Three** (page 64), discuss, and then fill in the similarities and differences between the three Isaiahs.

Wrapping It Up: (5 minutes) Students reflect on how confronting someone compassionately helps that person to maintain hope for a better future.

Chapter 6 • Lesson 3

Essential Question: What has enabled the Jewish people to keep Israel in our hearts for thousands of years?

Getting Started: (5 minutes) Remind students that Second Isaiah prophesied after the Babylonians destroyed Judah and exiled many Judeans to Babylonia. Students describe what they imagine life might have been like for the exiled Judeans and why they would have longed to return to Judea. List students' suggestions on the board.

Exploring the Text:

1. (5 minutes) Students individually write responses to the questions below **Comforting Those Far from Home** (page 64). Volunteers share their responses. Explain that students will study how Isaiah comforted the exiles.

2. (10 minutes) Partners read **Comforting Those Far from Home** (page 64). Students describe the condition of the exiles and suggest why Isaiah would want to comfort them and fill them with hope. Students discuss the importance of hope if we are to achieve our dreams. Volunteers take turns reading aloud one or two lines from **Isaiah 40:28–29, 42:6–7** (page 64) and explaining why those words would bring hope to the exiles.

3. (5 minutes) Write on the board: Who? What are they feeling? thinking? hoping? Students read silently the **passage based on Psalm 137 and Isaiah 40:27** (page 65). Students discuss the feelings, thoughts, and hopes of the exiles and Isaiah that seem evident from this text.

4. (10 minutes) Read aloud the first one and a half sentences of **Longing for Israel** (page 65). Lead students in a choral reading of Psalms 137:5–6. The class discusses the imagery portrayed by these phrases and how these verses convey the incomparable importance of Jerusalem. Students silently finish reading **Longing for Israel**. Students discuss how prayer may have helped to keep alive the dream to return to Jerusalem.

5. (5 minutes) Students read silently **Historical Note: The Fall of Judah** (page 66). Students refer to the list recorded during "Getting Started" and add additional information about the exiles' lives. Students identify the differences between the lives of those who remained in Judah and those who were exiled.

6. (5 minutes) Ask questions based on the **map** and on the **art** (page 66) to deepen students' understanding of the situation of the exiles. Suggested questions include: How far apart are Jerusalem and Babylon? (*approx. 700 miles*) What do you think it was like to live under another king? What emotions is the artist showing in Isaiah and in the people listening to him?

Wrapping It Up: (5 minutes) Students suggest which of Isaiah's messages found on pages 64–66 might have given the Israelites the greatest hope that they would return to Israel.

Chapter 6 • Isaiah: Righteous Spirit of Worship

Chapter 6 • Lesson 4

Essential Question: What does a "better world" look like?

Getting Started: (5 minutes) Students brainstorm what a "better world" might look like. Record their suggestions on the board. Students identify Jewish values and *mitzvot* that can guide us to work to build a "better world."

Exploring the Text:

1. (7 minutes) Students read silently the first paragraph of **Isaiah's Vision of a Better World** (page 67) and underline Isaiah's vision of how people should worship God. *(pursuing peace and justice)* Divide the class into small groups. Half of the groups discuss and write a response to the bolded questions; the other half discuss and write a response to the question below the **photograph of the two girls** (page 67). Groups present their thoughts to the class.

2. (5 minutes) Students individually read and complete **Skills for a Peaceful World** (page 67). Students share their answers with the class. Create a class list of skills or character traits shared by peacemakers.

3. (7 minutes) Lead the class in a choral reading of **Isaiah 2:3–4, 11:6** (page 67). Discuss the meaning of these verses. Students copy one or two lines onto a page, illustrate, and explain how these lines portray a better world. Display and/or scan and upload these pieces to your Prophets Web space.

4. (10 minutes) Partners read the remainder of **Isaiah's Vision of a Better World** (pages 67–68) and the caption below the **photo of Martin Luther King, Jr.** (page 68). Students discuss why Isaiah's words have rung true for centuries. If possible, play a recording of Dr. King's speech.

5. (5 minutes) Students read silently **God of All the Earth** (page 68) and underline Isaiah's vision of how people should worship God. Students individually write responses to the questions and then share responses with the class.

6. (10 minutes) Write on the board: If you will it, it is no dream. Students discuss this phrase and give examples to demonstrate its meaning. Partners read and complete **In the Footsteps of the Prophets: Theodor Herzl** (page 69). Students share their thoughts as to why both forms of justice are important. Teach, or invite the music specialist to teach, the students to sing Herzl's words in Hebrew, "Im Tirtzu."

Wrapping It Up: (10 minutes) Give everyone a "Vision Page" made up of the following questions: What is one good thing in your class, school, or synagogue that you would like to make even better? What would you like it to look like a year from now? What can you realistically do in the next six months? What can you realistically do in the next month? In small groups, students respond to the questions and develop a general plan to work toward making something good even better.

Chapter 7
Jeremiah: Persistent Voice of Teshuvah

Chapter Overview Jeremiah was born around 640 BCE in Judah. He spoke out against greed and corruption, proclaiming that ritual worship would not save the people of Judah; rather, they should live ethical lives. Furthermore, when the king of Judah chose to align with Egypt, Jeremiah challenged the king's authority, proclaiming that Judah should align with Babylonia. Because of his unpopular religious and political messages, Jeremiah was jailed twice and his life was threatened many times. Yet Jeremiah continued to speak up for justice and preach that people repent. The words of Jeremiah urge all of us to do *teshuvah* and to improve. The actions of Jeremiah remind us that we must each contribute to making the world a better place.

Core Concepts
- We are all capable of doing *teshuvah*—repentance.
- It is our responsibility to speak up for justice, even if our message is controversial or unpopular.
- One is not expected to finish the job, nor is one free to quit.

Learning Objectives Students will be able to:
- Define *teshuvah* and explain the importance of believing that people are able to change their ways. (Lesson 1)
- Suggest why people speak up for justice, despite risks and challenges, and why they are more likely to do so when they are in a safe, accepting environment. (Lesson 2)
- Explain the import of each of us doing our part—and being persistent—to make the world a better place. (Lesson 3)

Materials Needed Lesson 2—Two sets of question sheets based on **Jeremiah Puts His Life on the Line**. (Pages 73–75)

The Tech Connection Refer to the general suggestions on page 7. The following are additional ideas for your Web page or Wikispace about Jeremiah:
- List all the kings of Judah, including the approximate dates they ruled, and any prophets who lived at those times.
- Research and report on a modern day hero who, despite risks, speaks out for justice.
- Read about King Josiah and report on his work to bring about religious reforms.
- Upload artists' renditions of Jeremiah. Comment on what the artist is saying about the prophet.
- Upload or create links to video recordings of the song "Lo Alecha" (*Pirkei Avot* 2:21).
- Research and report on Natan Sharansky.

Chapter 7 • Lesson 1

Essential Question: How does believing that others are capable of teshuvah encourage us to speak up for justice?

Getting Started: (5 minutes) Explain that *teshuvah*, repentance, takes place when a person turns away from wrong and then, in a similar situation, does the right thing. Students give examples of a person doing *teshuvah*. Discuss why it is important that we believe a person can do *teshuvah*.

Exploring the Text:

1. (10 minutes) Partners read the **text based on Jeremiah 1:4–10** (page 70). Call on a pair of students to do a dramatic reading of the account. Ask: Why do you think the Bible records that Jeremiah felt lonely and different from others? Why would believing in *teshuvah* make it easier for Jeremiah to prophesy? How is Jeremiah's call to prophecy similar or different from the calls to prophecy of other prophets?

2. (15 minutes) Assign each student or pair of students one of the items listed in **Prophet's Profile: Jeremiah** (page 71). Students read their assigned item and write one idea they derive about Jeremiah from this item. For example, knowing that Jeremiah was born in 640 BCE informs us that he was living at the time of the first Holy Temple. Students read their item and their insight to the class. Students focus on Jeremiah's Major Contribution and discuss how his teaching allowed Judaism to survive in and out of Israel after the Temple was destroyed.

3. (5 minutes) Students read silently the first two paragraphs of **Kids Have What It Takes** (page 72). Students respond to the questions, explaining why they empathize more with Jeremiah or with Samuel.

4. (15 minutes) Partners read the midrash about Jeremiah complaining to God from **P'sikta Rabbati 26; Leviticus Rabbah 10:2** (page 72) and write responses to the questions following the midrash (page 73). Partners share their answers with the class. Students brainstorm a list of traits that make someone a strong prophet. Students discuss if Jeremiah's innocence and trust might help him to believe that others can and will do *teshuvah*.

    Students finish reading silently **Kids Have What It Takes** (page 73). Ask: How does believing that we have the ability—and the responsibility—motivate us to take on challenges?

Wrapping It Up: (10 minutes) Remind students that Jeremiah felt like a social outcast. Students discuss what it feels like to not fit in, identify actions or words that cause someone to feel like an outsider, then describe what *teshuvah* for ostracizing someone could look like. A volunteer reads the caption for the **photograph of the girls** (page 72). Students suggest how they can make their school a better place for all. Record students' suggestions and display them in your classroom and on the Web. Encourage students to follow these suggestions.

36 The Prophets: Speaking Out for Justice • Lesson Plan Manual

Chapter 7 • Lesson 2

Essential Question: What compels us to speak up for justice even when the message is controversial or unpopular?

Getting Started: (5 minutes) Students share examples from history, books, or films of a leader delivering a persuasive speech. Students explain why the person gave the speech and how it was received by the listeners. Students speculate why a person who is jeered by crowds would nonetheless deliver his or her message.

Exploring the Text:

1. (5 minutes) Divide the class into groups of 3–4 students. The groups read and discuss **Help! I Can't Stop Myself!** (page 72). Volunteers share their responses with the class. As a class, identify issues that your students believe in deeply.

2. (15 minutes) Give half of the groups sheets with the following questions: What was Jeremiah's problem? What did he want? Why did he want it? What did he do to get it? What do you think he will do next? Give the remaining groups these questions: What was the problem of the Judeans? What did they want? Why did they want it? What did they do to get it? What do you think they will do next?

   Groups read **Jeremiah Puts His Life on the Line** (pages 73–75), and discuss and record answers to the questions on their sheets. Representatives from each group identify the problems of the Judeans and of Jeremiah. Representatives then share what the Judeans and what Jeremiah wanted. Continue having groups compare the desires and actions of the Judeans and Jeremiah. Students predict what the Judeans and Jeremiah will do next. Write these predictions on the board.

   Students discuss why Jeremiah was compelled to deliver these prophecies despite the negative reception from the Judeans.

3. (10 minutes) Partners read **What Do You Think?** (page 73). Students discuss and write responses to the questions. Two sets of partners join to form a group of four students. Members of the group share their responses with one another.

4. (5 minutes) With the same group of four, students read the **text based on Jeremiah 26:8–16** (page 74). Students compare the text describing the Judeans' and Jeremiah's actions with their own predictions listed on the board.

5. (10 minutes) Students complete **Let's Make a Midrash** (page 76) and portray Jeremiah as he awaited the verdict of his trial. (Optional: Scan and upload students' work to your Prophets Web space.)

Wrapping It Up: (5 minutes) Students reflect on the experiences of Jeremiah and discuss the difference between speaking before people who are supportive and accepting, and those who disagree and are antagonistic. Students suggest how making the classroom a kinder place creates a safe environment for sharing one's views.

Chapter 7 • Lesson 3

Essential Question: Why take risks and work toward a goal that we may not achieve?

Getting Started: (5 minutes) Students share examples of a person, such as Herzl, who fought for a cause, helped move others to fight for it, but never saw the goal achieved. Students discuss why that person's work, though unfinished, was essential.

Exploring the Text:

1. (5 minutes) A volunteer reads **Historical Note: Judah Is Vulnerable** (page 75). Students refer to the **map** (page 77) and circle the kingdom of Israel, controlled by the Babylonians, and the kingdom of Egypt. Students discuss what Judeans may have been hoping for or were afraid of at that time.

2. (5 minutes) Write on the board: How did Jeremiah challenge the kings' authority? What were the consequences of his words? Partners read **A Prophet's Persistence** (pages 75 and 77) and share responses to the questions posted on the board. Students suggest ways Jeremiah might creatively deliver his messages.

3. (10 minutes) Six volunteers *(a narrator, Jeremiah, Baruch, two princes, and King Jehoiakim)* come to the front of the room to act out the **text based on Jeremiah 36** (page 78). Students explain why Jeremiah needed Baruch's help and suggest why Jeremiah and Baruch persisted in speaking out despite the risks involved. A student reads the caption next to the **art of Baruch and Jeremiah** (page 78). The class responds to the questions in the caption.

4. (5 minutes) Students read **Historical Note: The Destruction of Judah** (page 80) and consider how the political situation may have driven Jeremiah's commitment. A volunteer reads the caption next to the **photo of the people studying Torah** (page 80). Discuss when or why we may need to overlook our doubts.

5. (5 minutes) Partners read **Prayer Connection: Me or Us?** (page 79) and discuss which form of the pronouns speaks more powerfully to them.

6. (10 minutes) Students read the remainder of **A Prophet's Persistence** and **Success or Failure?** (pages 79–80) silently. Students discuss how a young person can help to improve the world.

7. (5 minutes) Partners read **In the Footsteps of the Prophets: Nathan Sharansky** (page 81) and compare Sharansky to Jeremiah.

Wrapping It Up: (5 minutes) Write the teaching from Pirkei Avot 2:21—"You are not expected to finish the job, but you are not free to quit"—on the board. Students discuss how the actions of Jeremiah and Sharansky demonstrate the truth of this statement. Students give examples of things they would like to work toward even though they cannot do the whole job alone. Teach, or have your music specialist teach, students to sing the Hebrew words of Pirkei Avot 2:21 put to music, "Lo Alecha."

The Prophets: Speaking Out for Justice • Lesson Plan Manual

Chapter 8
Jonah: Runaway Messenger of Mercy

Chapter Overview The story of Jonah is unlike that of any other prophet. When God commands Jonah to go to Nineveh to tell the people to repent, Jonah thinks he can flee from God and boards a ship to Tarshish. God has a great fish swallow Jonah. Jonah prays to God from the fish, is spewed onto dry ground, and then fulfills God's command to go to Nineveh, which is in Assyria—the kingdom that conquered Israel. Jonah, however, is distressed when the Ninevites repent. Jonah is seemingly a man who believes in strict justice—the wrongdoer must be punished. Yet God is merciful. God gives Jonah a second chance, God wants the Ninevites to repent, and God responds to Jonah with mercy when Jonah is angry that the Ninevites have been spared. This unusual prophetic book teaches the Jewish values of repentance and mercy, and encourages us to hope and believe that all people can change for the better.

Core Concepts

- The ancient words of the prophets continue to be personally meaningful for us today.
- Repentance and forgiveness allow us to become better people and to build a better world.
- Strict justice must be balanced by mercy.

Learning Objectives Students will be able to:

- Derive personally meaningful lessons from the Book of Jonah. (Lesson 1)
- Describe the Jewish view on repentance as demonstrated in the Book of Jonah. (Lesson 2)
- Explain why Jewish tradition teaches us to balance strict justice with mercy. (Lesson 3)

Materials Needed Lesson 1— slips of paper numbered 1–9 and a page of directions ("Create a skit in which someone asks you to do something you don't want to do, and you walk away. Create a second skit in which you are asked the same thing but resolve the conflict through conversation. Present your skits to the class."); Lesson 2— blank paper and envelopes.

The Tech Connection Refer to the general suggestions on page 7. The following are additional ideas for your Web page or Wikispace about Jonah:

- Upload art images from the Book of Jonah, such as Jonah in the fish, Jonah prophesying in Nineveh, and Jonah sitting under the plant. Focus on specific pieces of art and write what the artist may want us to learn about Jonah.
- Research and report on the history of Nineveh.
- Learn to chant, and then record, the opening verses of the Book of Jonah.
- Students write a midrashic ending to the account telling what Jonah does after God has explained why God wanted the Ninevites to repent.
- Research and report on Henrietta Szold and Hadassah.
- Upload the personal prayers students write on page 89.
- Research and report on the uses and meaning of "forty" in the bible. (Jonah preaches that Nineveh will be overthrown in forty days.)

Chapter 8 • Lesson 1

Essential Question: How do we derive personally meaningful lessons from an ancient account?

Getting Started: (5 minutes) Students brainstorm what they already know about the prophet Jonah. Review with students the important Jewish values they have learned from each of the prophets (refer to the **Values Index** on page 96 of student text). Ask students to suggest what Jewish values, or lessons, they might learn from Jonah. Write their suggestions on the board.

Exploring the Text:

1. (10 minutes) Write on the board: What do you find most surprising about this account? What is one lesson you learn from it? Partners read the **text based on Jonah 1:1–3:3** (pages 82 and 84) and write responses to the questions posted on the board. Students share their responses with the class. List the "Lessons Learned" on the board. Compare these lessons to the lessons students predicted in "Getting Started." Students discuss how Jonah may have felt when he was given a second chance, and why it is important for us to forgive and allow others a second chance.

2. (10 minutes) Students number the items in **Prophet's Profile: Jonah** (page 83) 1–9. Assign each student a "secret" item by giving each student a slip of paper with a number (1–9) written on it. Students silently read their assigned item and make up a clue about it. For example: My Hebrew name is connected with peace (#2). A volunteer comes to the front of the room and tells his or her clue. Classmates guess the item number. The student who guesses correctly reads the item description aloud and then comes to the front for others to guess his or her item. Students share which item they find most interesting and explain its interest.

3. (10 minutes) Divide the class into groups of 3–5 students. Groups read and share responses to **Walk or Talk?** (page 84). Give everyone directions (see Materials on page 39). Each group makes up and presents a two-part scenario in which they are asked to do something they do not want to do. In the first part, they walk away or ignore the request. In the second part, they resolve the conflict through dialogue. The class discusses the importance of open communication to resolve conflicts.

4. (5 minutes) Students read silently **A Surprisingly Great Story** (pages 84–85 and 87). Tell students they will return to the questions at the end of the unit.

5. (5 minutes) Partners read **Prayer Connection: An Early Thanksgiving** (page 85) and share responses to the questions following the text. As a class, students brainstorm one lesson they learned from this text. Add their suggestions to the "Lessons Learned" list on the board.

> **Wrapping It Up:** (10 minutes) A volunteer reads the caption next to the **photo of the "Understanding" sign** (page 86). Students share answers to the questions in the caption. Students suggest how studying a text, such as Jonah, in depth helps them to find personal meaning.

Chapter 8 • Lesson 2

Essential Question: Why is repentance an important Jewish value?

Getting Started: (5 minutes) Students think about a time when they were given a second chance. Students share how it felt knowing that they could apologize, change their behavior, and start again—that is, repent. Explain that the Book of Jonah tells of Jonah, the people of Nineveh, and even God repenting.

Exploring the Text:

1. (15 minutes) Divide the class into groups of 3–5 students. Groups read the first three paragraphs of **Repentance Wins the Day** (page 87) and write responses to the questions. A member of each group shares its responses with the class.

2. (5 minutes) A volunteer reads the caption next to the **art depicting Jonah** (page 87) and then leads the class in a choral reading of Jonah's prophecy. Students suggest what Jonah may have hoped or expected would happen after his declaration.

3. (10 minutes) Students meet again in groups and read the **account based on Jonah 3** (page 86). Direct half of the groups to list reasons why Jonah would be pleased when the Ninevites and God repent, and the other half to list reasons why he would be upset by their repentance. Representatives from each group share their lists with the class. Students predict whether they think Jonah will or will not be pleased that his prophecy was heeded. Record students' predictions for reference. Students suggest how this account teaches us that repentance is an important Jewish value.

4. (10 minutes) Students read silently the next four paragraphs of **Repentance Wins the Day** (page 88). Discuss the questions about accepting imperfections in all of us. Students share how it is sometimes difficult to change behaviors. Guide students to acknowledge that it is natural for change to be difficult and/or slow, but that that should not deter us from trying to be better.

5. (5 minutes) Partners read the final three paragraphs of **Repentance Wins the Day** (pages 88–89). Students discuss the closing questions and write one lesson they learn from **Repentance Wins the Day**. Students share their "lessons learned." A volunteer reads **What Do You Think?** (page 89), and students discuss the significance of God sending a prophet to a future enemy.

6. (5 minutes) A volunteer reads the caption below the **photograph of the girl with the older couple** (page 88). Students respond to the questions in the caption.

Wrapping It Up: (10 minutes) Give each student a sheet of paper and an envelope. Students privately write something about themselves that they would like to change for the better. Encourage students to record steps they can take to become better, including if they need to apologize to or forgive someone. Students place their writing in an envelope and seal the envelope. Collect the envelopes and arrange to have the envelopes returned to the students in the fall.

Chapter 8 • Lesson 3

Essential Question: Why is being merciful an important Jewish value?

Getting Started: (5 minutes) A volunteer comes to the front of the room and acts out "begging for mercy." Students describe what it means to treat someone with mercy. Tell students that in this lesson they will look at what the Book of Jonah teaches us about the importance of being merciful.

Exploring the Text:

1. (5 minutes) Read aloud the opening sentences of **God's Prayer** (page 89). Lead students in a choral reading of God's prayer from the Talmud. Students respond to the first two questions after the prayer and discuss what this prayer teaches us about the Jewish view of mercy and compassion. Consider setting aside time at the end of the lesson to have students write personal prayers.

2. (10 minutes) Remind students that in the last lesson they predicted Jonah's response to the repentance of the Ninevites. Take a quick vote of who thinks Jonah will be pleased and who thinks he will be unhappy. Write on the board: How does Jonah feel? What is surprising about this account? What does this account teach us about the Jewish view on mercy? Partners read the opening paragraphs of **Will We Listen or Turn Away?** (page 89) and the **text based on Jonah 4** (page 90). Partners discuss their responses to the questions on the board. As a class, students share their responses.

3. (5 Minutes) Students continue reading silently **Will We Listen or Turn Away** (page 91). As a class, students discuss the meaning of strict justice and explain, and offer examples to demonstrate, why strict justice must be balanced with mercy.

4. (5 minutes) A volunteer reads the caption below the **photograph of the infant's feet** (page 91). Students discuss the questions about the portrayal of God included in the caption. Inform students that in some of our prayers we call God *Avinu Malkeinu*, meaning "Our Father [or Parent], Our Ruler." Students discuss how this name reflects our relationship with God and how we hope God will deal with us.

5. (10 minutes) Write on the board: What Jewish values do we learn from the Book of Jonah? Divide the class into groups of 3–5 students. Groups finish reading **Will We Listen or Turn Away?** (page 92), write a list of values in response to the question on the board, and share their lists with the class.

6. (10 minutes) Students read silently **In the Footsteps of the Prophets: Henrietta Szold** (page 93) and write two Jewish values that may have inspired Szold. Students share, and explain, their responses.

Wrapping It Up: (5 minutes) Students return to the questions on pages 84 and 85 and discuss why we read the Book of Jonah on Yom Kippur and what this account teaches us about godliness.

Constructing Personal Meaning from The Prophets: Speaking Out for Justice

Devote one or two classes to reviewing *The Prophets: Speaking Out for Justice*. There are many ways you may choose to review. Here are a few suggestions:

1. **Students review the teachings of the prophets to construct and present a case for studying the prophets of the Bible.**

    Divide the class into groups of 3–5. Give everyone a page with these written directions:

    Your task is to prepare a presentation that will convince others of the importance of studying the prophets of the Bible. Ideas to present include: Short biographies of some of the great prophets; descriptions of why they were famous; explanations of the lessons and values we learn from the prophets, individually and collectively; fun and interesting facts about the prophets; how the prophets inspire us to speak up for justice.

    Be creative and have fun with your presentation. Your group might, for example, put on a skit, write a song, and/or design a poster. Your presentation should demonstrate that you are familiar with the great prophets of Israel and the lessons we learn from them.

    You might devote one class session to planning and a second one to presentations.

2. **Students address essential questions related to the teachings of the prophets.**

    Choose 5–7 Essential Questions taken from the opening of each lesson. Divide class into groups of 3-5. Prepare written directions as follows:

    Choose one of the Essential Questions listed below and prepare a written response to it. Include in your response (i) references to at least one of the prophets we have studied and (ii) examples from history or personal experience that support your answer. The Essential Questions to choose from are: [list of 5–7 Essential Questions]

    A representative from your group will present your response to the class.

    Review the qualities of an Essential Question and remind students that each lesson has been guided by an Essential Question. Give each student a page with the written directions. Allow groups 3 minutes to choose an Essential Question and 20 minutes to prepare a response. A representative from one group presents its response. If another group has chosen the same question, their group shares its thoughts. Students share additional thoughts on this same question.

    Groups take turns presenting their response to an Essential Question. If time allows, establish new groups that will, again, choose and respond to an Essential Question.

3. **The Tech Connection** If your class has developed a Web site, devote a class session to reviewing your class's work. Celebrate everyone's contributions. If the site is publicly accessible, ask students' permission to send the link to the director of education and the rabbi. Discuss with students whether they would like to share the link with their families. All students need to be comfortable with this.

Assessments

You can assess your students' work in a wide variety of ways. Students might, for example, prepare a project, present a skit, design an action figure, or write a song that reflects the life and teachings of one of the prophets.

Below you will find a set of recall as well as open-ended questions to use at the end of each chapter. The questions largely focus on big ideas, themes, concepts, and understandings. They are designed to have the students reflect on the life and teachings of each prophet and consider how the prophets inspire us to speak out for justice. You may choose to adapt or create your own questions. Alternatively, you may wish to give students the option of choosing just a few of the questions.

Moses: Radical Shepherd of Israel

(Suggestions for possible answers are included in parentheses.)

1. Describe two ways that Moses's occupation may have prepared him to lead the Israelites. *(As a shepherd, Moses would have to be patient and compassionate. Needing to care for and guide sheep may have prepared Moses to lead and care for the Israelites as they journeyed in the desert.)*

2. Explain how Moses's upbringing, from birth through his teens, may have helped him to understand both the Israelite and the Egyptian people. *(As a very young child, Moses learned about his own people, the Israelites, from his mother and family. Once he was brought back by Pharaoh's daughter, he lived among the Egyptians, learning their culture.)*

3. List four of the women who saved Moses's life, describe their roles in his being saved, and identify a Jewish value we learn from their actions. *(Shifrah and Puah defied Pharaoh's order to kill all the Israelite boys at birth; Moses's mother placed him in a basket on the bank of the River Nile; Moses's sister watched the baby until he was safe; Pharaoh's daughter drew him from the water and raised him as her son. We learn about compassion from each of their actions.)*

4. What does it mean that we are a "kingdom of priests"? *(All of us are holy.)* List two responsibilities we have because we are a "kingdom of priests." *(We must perform acts of kindness; it is our responsibility to pursue justice; we must be fair and truthful.)*

5. Why did Moses establish a judicial system? *(He listened to his father-in-law's advice; he alone had been settling all the daily disputes—the new system offered community support and reduced his work.)* Do you think the Israelites liked this new system? Explain why or why not. *(Yes, because they would have more people to speak to regarding a problem; they would not have to wait as long for a judicial decision. No, because each person wanted Moses's opinion, not another Israelite's.)*

6. How does Moses respond to the complaining of the Israelites? *(He remains loyal to his people; he helps them develop the maturity and resolve to take on the duties of freedom.)* What do we learn from Moses when we read how he continues to lead them despite their complaints? *(Leadership requires commitment and patience; a leader needs to be compassionate and show understanding.)*

Samuel: Reluctant Kingmaker

1. What is a Jewish value Samuel may have learned from either Hannah or Eli? Describe what Hannah or Eli did or said that may have taught Samuel this value. *(Samuel may have learned to have faith and trust in God from Hannah. Hannah showed her faith when she asked God for a son, dedicated her son's life to the service of God, and brought him to live at the temple with Eli; Samuel may have learned about being faithful to and worshipping God as Samuel worked alongside Eli at the temple.)*

2. Why was Samuel against having a human king rule Israel? *(Samuel believed that Israel's God was the One and Only Ruler. He did not want Israelites serving any human being; Samuel felt that a king would oppress the Israelites through heavy taxes and military service.)* Explain why you think he was right or wrong to feel this way. *(Open-ended question. I think Samuel was right because the tribes should have been able to join forces without having a king over them; I think he was wrong because the tribes were weak and they needed a strong leader to unite them and make them stronger.)*

3. Why did the Israelites want a king? *(Their survival was threatened by the surrounding enemy nations. They needed a ruler who would unite and arm the tribes.)* If you were an Israelite, would you have wanted a king? Why or why not? *(Open-ended question. I would have wanted a king because all the nations around us had kings and I think a king could unite us and give us power. I would not have wanted a king because I believe the Israelites should serve only God.)*

4. Give an example of an account from the Book of Samuel that reminds us that we are partners with God. *(The Israelites joined forces and fought against the Philistines. They did not simply rely on God, or the Ark, to protect them; Adonai told Samuel whom he should anoint. Samuel then anointed Saul to be king.)* Name something you can do as a partner with God. *(Open-ended question. Fulfill the mitzvah of feeding the hungry by making sandwiches for the homeless; fulfill the mitzvah of clothing the poor [the naked] by donating used clothing.)*

5. What does the history of the early kings of Israel teach us about the need for a balance of power? *(Kingdoms are weakened when one person is given too much power; in ancient Israel, the joint leadership of kings, priests, and prophets supported a balance of power.)* Give an example to support your answer. *(Solomon had heavily taxed the population and required forced labor—making many Israelites unhappy. After his death, people rebelled and the kingdom of Israel split in two; in ancient Israel the priests performed the sacrifices, while the prophets instructed all the people—including the king. The king was the civil ruler; the priests and prophets were the religious rulers.)*

6. What value or teaching in the Book of Samuel do you find most personally meaningful? *(trust and faith in people and in God; we are partners with God.)* Explain why this value is important to you.

Elijah: Zealous Critic of the King

1. Give an example of Elijah demonstrating courage. *(Elijah confronted King Ahab and his non-Israelite wife Jezebel for their evil ways. He spoke out against the Israelites, asking them how long they would worship both Adonai and Baal; Elijah told King Ahab that because he and Jezebel had plotted the death of an innocent man, dogs would lap up his blood and devour Jezebel, too.)* What do you learn about the Jewish value of courage from the accounts of Elijah? *(Open-ended. It often takes courage to do what is right; it is important to fight for justice, even if it takes courage to do so.)*

2. What are some qualities of Elijah that make him a good leader? *(He was committed to his beliefs; he had faith in God; he was courageous.)* Describe an event or an action in which Elijah demonstrated this quality. *(Elijah fought against the prophets of Baal and Asherah; Elijah spoke out against the Israelites, letting them know they were wrong to worship Baal along with Adonai.)*

3. Name someone you admire, either from history or today, who, like Elijah, spoke up in pursuit of justice. *(Dr. Martin Luther King, Jr.; Bella Abzug; Abraham Lincoln.)* Briefly describe what the person did and why you admire him or her.

4. Describe two traditions we follow today that include or refer to Elijah. *(The cup of Elijah on the seder table; opening the door for Elijah at the seder; singing "Eliyahu Hanavi" at havdalah.)* Why do you think Elijah has remained such an important figure in our tradition? *(Open-ended. According to tradition, Elijah never died—rather he was carried up to heaven in a fiery chariot. We imagine Elijah coming down from heaven and helping us make a better world. The values that Elijah has come to represent, such as justice and faith, are as essential today as they were in his day.)*

5. Name a Jewish ritual that connects us to godliness. *(Hearing a shofar sounded on Rosh Hashanah and Yom Kippur; participating in a Passover seder.)* Explain how this ritual may help you to hear and follow your conscience. *(Hearing a shofar reminds us that while no one is perfect, each of us can work to do our best; participating in a Passover seder reminds us to invite guests and "all who are hungry" to our table.)*

6. Explain why we are able to learn Jewish values from both historical events and traditional stories. *(Open-ended. Stories are often used to teach a moral or a value. We can learn an important value, such as honesty, from a fictional story. Similarly, an account in the bible need not be historical to serve as the basis for teaching a Jewish value.)*

Amos: Faithful Friend of the Covenant

1. What do you think was Amos's greatest challenge? Why was it so challenging? *(Going north to prophesy in Israel. This was challenging because Amos was a sheep breeder and farmer and needed to confront the wealthy city dwellers of the north; standing before the Israelites and prophesying that their kingdom would be destroyed. Perhaps he was afraid of how the people might react.)*

2. What is the meaning of "Let justice flow like water, righteousness like a mighty stream"? *(Justice should flow steadily, smoothly, endlessly. Righteousness should be a powerful, steady, limitless force.)* Do you think these words are still true today? Why or why not? *(Open-ended. Yes, because justice and righteousness are still, and will always be, essential in our lives.)*

3. Describe one thing Amos did that can inspire us today to influence others to live ethically. *(He asked our ancestors to repent by living righteous lives; he informed people of the consequences of their actions and then prayed for God to forgive them.)*

4. Give an example of Amos stepping out of his comfort zone. *(He confronted people who were more powerful than him, both socially and politically.)* What do we learn from this action? *(That we may need to step out of our own comfort zone to work toward a better world.)*

5. What were some of the wrongdoings of the Israelites? *(They prayed to false gods; they betrayed righteous people for the sake of silver; they mistreated the poor.)* Why would Amos want them to repent and for God to forgive, not punish, them? *(If the people would repent, the world would be a better place and the Israelites would once again serve Adonai. It is better for people to change and do the right thing than to be punished and not change their ways.)* Explain why you agree or disagree with Amos.

6. Name one Jewish value we learn from Amos. *(Speaking up for social justice.)* Give an example of how you can uphold that value. *(Speak up and let peers know they need to include a classmate who has been left out of a social event.)*

Isaiah: Righteous Spirit of Worship

1. Give an example of Isaiah being compassionate. *(When the Israelites were in exile, Isaiah prophesied that God was ready to forgive the exiles; Isaiah told the exiles that they would be returned to their homeland if they would repent.)* Explain why it is important to be compassionate when confronting someone who has committed a wrongdoing. *(Open-ended. When we are compassionate, the other person may be more willing to listen to us.)*

2. Who in the Book of Isaiah says "*Kadosh, kadosh, kadosh*"? *(Seraphim—winged angels.)* What do we do as we chant those words today? *(Rise up on our toes.)* Why do you think we do these motions? *(To feel as if we are reaching up toward God.)*

3. Identify one wrongdoing Isaiah spoke up against. *(Mistreating orphans; mistreating widows; rulers who are thieves.)* What is a similar, modern-day example of a wrongdoing that you would speak up against? *(Today we speak out against the mistreatment of the poor and of minority groups; we also speak out when there is corruption among our political leaders.)*

4. How does Isaiah describe a religious person? *(For Isaiah, a religious Jew is a Jew who cares for those who are vulnerable—the orphaned, widowed, poor, ill, oppressed, and elderly. We learn that "religious" does not mean simply performing rituals; rather it refers to pursuing justice.)*

5. Name one similarity between the actions or words of Theodore Herzl and those of Isaiah. *(They both spoke out about injustices carried out against people.)* Identify a Jewish value and describe how Herzl's work reflects that value. *(Herzl's work to create a Jewish homeland was motivated by the Jewish value of the pursuit of justice. Herzl believed the unjust treatment of the Jews would end only with the creation of a Jewish homeland.)*

6. Describe two of Isaiah's visions for a better world. *("They shall beat their swords into plowshares"; "nation shall not raise sword against nation"; "the wolf shall live with the lamb.")* Do you think these visions still hold true for today? Explain. *(Open-ended. Yes, because we are still hoping for peace.)*

Jeremiah: Persistent Voice of Teshuvah

1. Why did Jeremiah make so many enemies? *(He delivered unpopular religious and political messages.)* Do you think a leader must be willing to make enemies? Explain. *(Open-ended. Yes, because if you worry about pleasing everyone you will not have the courage to deliver an unpopular message.)*

2. How did the Judeans react when Jeremiah said that God's word—not worship at the Temple—was the true foundation of their religion? *(They gasped.)* Why did they respond this way? *(He was challenging their belief that ritual worship alone was enough to save them. Jeremiah was claiming that they also had to live ethical lives.)*

3. What Jewish value do we learn from reading about Jeremiah prophesying even though his message was controversial? *(To follow truth; pursue justice.)*

4. How did Jeremiah manage to speak out even when he was in hiding? *(His scribe and loyal partner, Baruch, wrote down all of Jeremiah's words and read them on Jeremiah's behalf.)* What do we learn from Jeremiah about commitment? *(Open-ended. When we are committed to a cause, we will find a way to succeed.)*

5. What is the Hebrew word for repentance? *(Teshuvah)* Why is repentance such an important Jewish value? *(Open-ended. By encouraging people to do teshuvah, we encourage people to do the right thing and, ultimately, to build a better world. It is important for people to know that they can change their ways for the better.)*

6. What is a connection between the work of Jeremiah and the rabbinic teaching, "You are not expected to finish the job, but you are not free to quit"? *(Jeremiah was not able to "finish his work," that is, to persuade the kingdom of Judah to accept God's teachings. Yet his words have guided us for centuries. His words continue to teach us today, reminding us that we can do teshuvah and work to do better.)* Describe one way that you fulfill the words of this teaching. *(Open-ended. I can collect canned food for the local food pantry.)*

Jonah: Runaway Messenger of Mercy

1. What do you find most surprising about the story of Jonah? *(Jonah tried to run away from God; Jonah went to sleep on the ship during a raging storm; the foreign sailors feared Adonai.)* Why do you find it surprising? *(I would think a prophet would carry out God's command and would know a person can't run from God; I can't imagine going to sleep on a boat that might sink; it's unusual that the foreign sailors immediately feared Adonai.)*

2. When is the Book of Jonah read in the synagogue? *(On Yom Kippur afternoon.)* Why do you think it is read on that day? *(On Yom Kippur we are thinking about repentance, and repentance is a main theme in the Book of Jonah.)*

3. What does the book of Jonah teach about the Jewish value of repentance? *(That everyone is capable of repentance.)* Describe a part of the story that teaches this. *(Jonah is given a second chance, and then goes to prophesy in Nineveh; the Ninevites immediately believe in God and repent.)*

4. What is unusual about Jonah going to Nineveh to prophesy? *(Nineveh is in Assyria—the kingdom that destroyed the Kingdom of Israel in 722 BCE.)* What do we learn from this event? *(We hope that even our greatest enemy will repent. We desire repentance, not punishment.)*

5. What does God's treatment of Jonah and of the Ninevites teach us about the Jewish value of mercy? *(That it is a Jewish value to show mercy and to forgive.)* Give an example of God treating either the Ninevites or Jonah with mercy. *(God sent Jonah ahead to warn the Ninevites of their destruction. Seeing that they repented, God decided not to destroy them; God had a great fish swallow Jonah, and had the fish spit Jonah back to safety on dry land. God gave Jonah a second chance.)*

6. Did Jonah believe in strict justice, mercy, or a combination of both? *(Strict justice.)* Give an example demonstrating why it is essential to balance strict justice with mercy. *(If we believe that everyone should be punished for a mistake, people would be less likely to try to change their ways; we learn from our mistakes. For the world to be a better place, we must be willing to forgive people and allow them to change for the better.)*